SURRENDER

BEING A MAN WHO HAS THE COURAGE
TO LIVE BEYOND HIS FEARS

JOE WELLS, M.MIN.

SURRENDER: BEING A MAN WHO HAS THE COURAGE TO LIVE BEYOND HIS FEARS
Copyright © 2023 by Kaio Publications
http://www.kaiopublications.org

All rights reserved. No part of this publication may be reproduced, stored in a retrieval system, or transmitted in any form by any means, electronic, mechanical, photocopy, recording, or otherwise, without the prior permission of the author, except as provided for by USA copyright law.

First printing 2023
Printed in the United States of America

Scripture quotations taken from the New American Standard Bible® (NASB), Copyright © 1960, 1962, 1963, 1968, 1971, 1972, 1973, 1975, 1977, 1995 by The Lockman Foundation
Used by permission. www.Lockman.org.

ISBN: 978-1-952955-44-0

Grammar edited by Tonja McRady
Cover and interior design by Kristin Arbuckle

TO THOSE WITH THE COURAGE
TO WAVE THE WHITE FLAG —
CHOOSING LIFE OVER DEATH.

TABLE OF CONTENTS

CHAPTER 1: SURRENDER TO HIS GOSPEL
- Briefing — 7
- Intel — 10
- Wrap-up — 19
- Field Notes — 20

CHAPTER 2: SURRENDER TO HIS PURPOSE
- Briefing — 23
- Intel — 27
- Wrap-up — 36
- Field Notes — 38

CHAPTER 3: SURRENDER TO HIS PURSUITS
- Briefing — 41
- Intel — 44
- Wrap-up — 55
- Field Notes — 56

CHAPTER 4: SURRENDER TO HIS WILL
- Briefing — 59
- Intel — 64
- Wrap-up — 81
- Field Notes — 82

CHAPTER 5: SURRENDER TO HIS MIGHTY HAND
- Briefing — 85
- Intel — 89
- Wrap-up — 102
- Field Notes — 106

"THUS, IN ONE SENSE, THE ROAD BACK TO GOD IS A ROAD OF MORAL EFFORT, OF TRYING HARDER AND HARDER. BUT IN ANOTHER SENSE, IT IS NOT TRYING THAT IS EVER GOING TO BRING US HOME. ALL THIS TRYING LEADS UP TO THE VITAL MOMENT AT WHICH YOU TURN TO GOD AND SAY, "YOU MUST DO THIS. I CAN'T.""

- C.S. LEWIS [1]

BRIEFING — SURRENDER TO HIS GOSPEL

Recently, while talking with my son about being a disciple of Jesus, he said something during our discussion that struck me, causing me to stop and think. He expressed the sentiment I've heard from many people regarding how we will never be "good enough" in following Jesus. To that point, he is correct; however, that was not the point that caused me to pause and reflect. It wasn't until he stressed that we must give Jesus our "best" in our walk and trust in the grace of God along the way. Like a car that abruptly brakes, that's when my mind halted.

It caused me to pause because it hit me. This mindset of "giving God my best" has taken hold in the church and society. With our desire to be pleasing to God and bring Him honor and glory, we have adopted a mentality that emphasizes us as the disciples.

Us giving God our best...is it possible this premise is incomplete?

I'm not making a case for the extreme opposite of this statement that says since we can't be good enough, why even try to be and do what God desires? That belief is flat-out wrong and rebellious. Instead, I'm making the case that when the emphasis in our walk with God is that we do our best, the fulcrum or the hinge of that statement is on us, and that's never where it should ultimately rest. What if, instead of saying we need to give God our best, we say we need to be disciples who surrender every aspect of our lives to Him?

In other words, instead of God wanting my best, He wants my total surrender. What does that really look like and mean?

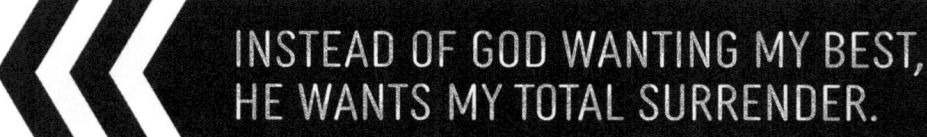

INSTEAD OF GOD WANTING MY BEST, HE WANTS MY TOTAL SURRENDER.

Merriam-Webster.com defines *surrender* as "the action of yielding one's person or giving up the possession of something especially into the power of another."[2] Chances are, you've seen this in images of soldiers waving a white flag in surrender as they lay their weapons down, deciding to no longer resist or put up a fight. You may have even watched a movie where an officer rode under the protection of the white flag to discuss terms of surrender with a more powerful foe. I'll never forget seeing images on television as a middle school kid of Iraqi soldiers with hands held high in the air coming toward the American military. Some were holding white pieces of cloth after American forces swiftly and with great power rushed to the aid of Kuwait after Saddam Hussain's army invaded.

But when did the white flag become a symbol of surrender?

Historians generally conclude that this symbol of surrender began in the East during the Han Dynasty's rule in China (A.D. 25-220) over 2000 years ago. However, on a separate front, in the West there is documentation from historians such as the Roman historian Cornelius Tacitus who, in A.D. 109, documented this practice was known and utilized during the Second Battle of Cremona in A.D. 69.

Some of the legionaries were already forming up for the 'tortoise' and others discharging missiles and stones, when the morale of the Vitellians gradually began to crack. The higher the rank, the less the will to resist the inevitable. They feared that if Cremona too were taken by storm, there would be no further question of quarter and the conqueror's anger would fall entirely upon the tribunes and centurions who were worth killing rather than upon the multitude who had nothing to lose. But the ordinary soldier stood firm, for he cared nothing for the future and thought himself relatively safe, because unknown. Roaming through the streets or hidden in houses, these men refused to ask for peace even when they had ceased to wage war. The camp commandants took down the portraits of Vitellius and the indications of his name. Caecina, who was still in confinement, was released from his shackles and requested to plead for the Vitellians. He stood on his dignity and refused, but they wore down his resistance with tearful entreaties, presenting the degrading phenomenon of many fine soldiers invoking the aid of a single traitor. Soon after, **the white flag was displayed prominently from the walls.** *Antonius signalled the cease-fire, and the Vitellians brought out the standards and eagles. These were followed by a dejected column of disarmed men with downcast eyes. The victors had formed up to receive them, and at first jeered and thrust at them with their weapons. But after a while, when the beaten men faced their insults without flinching and impassively endured everything, their tormentors remembered that this was the army which, not long previously, had refrained from pressing home its victory at Bedriacum. But when Caecina, distinguished by bordered toga and lictors, thrust aside the throng and made his way forward in his capacity as consul, the victors* *were in an uproar. They taunted him with conceit and malevolence, never attractive vices, and treachery as well. Antonius intervened, and giving him an escort sent him off to Vespasian (emp. added).*[3]

This practice became so well-known and practiced that treaties such as the Hague Conventions of 1899 and 1907 and the Geneva Convention signed in 1949 included it in their language as an acceptable way to communicate surrender from one military to another. To fly a white flag of surrender, only to turn and attack or act contrary to what the white flag means, is considered a serious military crime worthy of severe punishment. Even to this day, the waving of the white flag communicates complete surrender.

So, to say God desires and deserves our complete surrender is not the same as saying He wants our very best. In one, we wave the white flag and submit to God. In the other, while we have good motives and intent, the effort we put forth is the measuring stick of effectiveness. Surrender is far better; however, where does it begin?

INTEL >>> SURRENDER TO HIS GOSPEL

I don't know if you've ever considered yourself an enemy combatant, but that is precisely the title worn by those who oppose God. I'm not suggesting you are currently in this position today; however, in Romans 3:23, we learn that every one of us at one time wore this treacherous title. Consider what the apostle Paul wrote in Romans 5:10 regarding this horrible state,

> *For if while we were **enemies** we were reconciled to God through the death of His Son, much more, having been reconciled, we shall be saved by His life (emp. added).*

It would do us well in better understanding this enemy combatant to understand this is not an idle word, nor does it denote a passive ignorance that causes one to stand in opposition. What Paul tells the Christians in Rome is that, as sinners who are helpless and hopeless, they once stood in hostile defiance before God. Just as Goliath opposed David, the prophets of Baal opposed Elijah, and the Pharisees opposed Jesus Christ, so we as non-Christians were enemy combatants who opposed God. James emphasized this as well in his writing when he penned,

> *You adulteresses, do you not know that friendship with the world is hostility toward God? Therefore, whoever wishes to be a friend of the world makes himself an **enemy** of God (Jas. 4:4, emp. added).*

In Acts chapter 13, we learn of an enemy combatant at the beginning of the first missionary journey of Paul and Barnabas. While on the island of Cyprus, they encountered Sergius Paulus after traversing the entire island and spreading the good news of the Gospel of Jesus Christ. He is described as the proconsul and a man of intelligence (v. 7). Unfortunately, they also encountered a Jewish false prophet, the enemy combatant Elymas the magician (v. 8). This evil man was actively opposing Paul and Barnabas as he stubbornly attempted to turn the proconsul away from the faith. We learn that Paul did not mince words nor sugarcoat the truth in his confrontation with this enemy of God.

> *But Saul, who was also known as Paul, filled with the Holy Spirit, fixed his gaze on him, and said," You who are full of all deceit and fraud, you son of the devil, you **enemy** of all righteousness, will you not cease to make crooked the straight ways of the Lord?' (vs. 9-10, emp. added).*

Throughout Scripture, we continually read about what happens to those who oppose God and His Word. Rebellion, pride, selfishness, stifling the advancement of truth, and numerous other attempts to thwart the elevating of God and His Word all come crashing down. God didn't tolerate these in the days of Moses. He didn't stand for them in the days of David. He did not wink at them in the days of Peter or Paul, and He won't overlook them now. Consider the following promises that have been and will continue to be fulfilled against those who oppose God.

- **Nahum 1:2:** "*A jealous and avenging God is the Lord; The Lord is avenging and wrathful. The Lord takes vengeance on His adversaries, And He reserves wrath for His enemies.*"
- **1 Samuel 2:10:** "*Those who contend with the Lord will be shattered; Against them He will thunder in the heavens....*"
- **Hosea 7:13:** "*Woe to them, for they have strayed from Me! Destruction is theirs, for they have rebelled against Me! I would redeem them, but they speak lies against Me.*"
- **Romans 1:18:** "*For the wrath of God is revealed from heaven against all ungodliness and unrighteousness of men who suppress the truth in unrighteousness....*"
- **John 3:36:** "*He who believes in the Son has eternal life; but he who does not obey the Son will not see life, but the wrath of God abides on him.*"

At first reading, you might find it odd to begin answering the question of the beginning of surrender by addressing the issue of enemy combatants; however, it is fundamental that we understand the battle. God and His truth are on one side, and sin and those who bask in it are on the other. These two sides are not close in agreement, and they are as far opposed to one another as possible. The war is ugly, and the consequences are real. However, no matter how staunchly the side of sin and those who are the enemies of God resist and dig in, they will never overcome God and the truth of His Word (1 Pet. 1:25).

> **THE WAR IS UGLY AND THE CONSEQUENCES ARE REAL.** »»

So, if victory is not possible for the enemy combatants opposing God, what is the answer? They can continue to resist; however, the Holy Spirit makes it very clear through the pen of the apostle Paul that God will,

> *...repay with affliction those who afflict you, and to give relief to you who are afflicted and to us as well when the Lord Jesus will be revealed from heaven with His mighty angels in flaming fire, dealing out retribution to those who do not know God and to those who do not obey the Gospel of our Lord Jesus. These will pay the penalty of eternal destruction, away from the presence of the Lord and from the glory of His power...* (2 Thess. 1:6-9).

In other words, for the enemies of God, defeat is inevitable. Because this is the case, the only logical answer, the only response that will save, the only soul-saving move is to wave the white flag of surrender in submission to the Gospel of Jesus Christ. Only in this surrender can God's grace and mercy appease God's wrath. In this surrender, the enemy of God becomes a child of God, the lost are saved, and the dead are made alive. This isn't just another event in the life of the redeemed; this is their transferred moment that changes everything (Col. 1:13).

As we turn our attention specifically to 1 Peter 1, we encounter a collection of people who have decided that being for God is far better than being against Him. They have waved the white flag of surrender in submitting to the Gospel of Jesus Christ. Peter reminds them of these when he writes regarding their surrender,

> *Since you have in obedience to the truth purified your souls for a sincere love of the brethren, fervently love one another from the heart, for you have been born again not of seed which is perishable but imperishable, that is, through the living and enduring word of God* (1 Pet. 1:22- 23).

He explains the connection further when he declares that the Gospel of Jesus Christ was preached to them in verse 12. Then in verse 25, he removes all doubt that the Word of God, the imperishable seed, the living, and the enduring Word, is what has been preached to them. As Peter draws the reader back to Isaiah 40:6-8, he emphasizes the enduring nature of the Word of God, encouraging the reader to rest in the certainty of what God has promised in His Word.

What is the message preached in the Gospel? In a quick search, we will find the Greek word for *Gospel*—εὐαγγέλιον—occurs in some form 101 times. Seventy-five of those times, the term is used in reference specifically to the good news of Jesus Christ. The other 26 times, the word is used to denote the preaching or proclamation of the good news. To better understand this good news, consider the following brief study of the Gospel found in the New Testament. What is the message preached?

 **THE GOSPEL IS THE MESSAGE...**

- **Acts 20:24—of the grace of God**
  - *"But I do not consider my life of any account as dear to myself, so that I may finish my course and the ministry which I received from the Lord Jesus, to testify solemnly of the gospel of the grace of God."*
- **2 Corinthians 4:4—of the glory of Christ**
  - *"...In whose case the god of this world has blinded the minds of the unbelieving so that they might not see the light of the gospel of the glory of Christ, who is the image of God."*
- **Ephesians 6:15—of peace**
  - *"...And having shod your feet with the preparation of the gospel of peace...."*
- **Colossians 1:23—of hope**
  - *"...If indeed you continue in the faith firmly established and steadfast, and not moved away from the hope of the gospel that you have heard, which was proclaimed in all creation under heaven, and of which I, Paul, was made a minister."*
- **Ephesians 1:13—of truth (see also Col. 1:5)**
  - *"In Him, you also, after listening to the message of truth, the gospel of your salvation—having also believed, you were sealed in Him with the Holy Spirit of promise,"*

- **2 Timothy 1:10**—of life and immortality
    - *"...But now has been revealed by the appearing of our Savior Christ Jesus, who abolished death and brought life and immortality to light through the gospel...."*

As we better understand our condition as the enemy combatant before waving the white flag of surrender in submission to the Gospel of Jesus Christ and we begin to see the bigger picture of the message preached surrounding the death, burial, and resurrection of Jesus Christ, we see our condition change from spiritually dead. Those who at one time had no hope now have hope. Those who were at one time not called people of God now are the children of God (1 Peter 2:10).

In 1 Peter 1, we read of three important blessings of surrendering to the Gospel of Jesus Christ.

 1. WHEN WE SURRENDER, WE ARE BORN AGAIN TO A LIVING HOPE

In John 3, Jesus explained to Nicodemus that *"unless one is born again, he cannot see the kingdom of God"* (v. 3). The logical response from Nicodemus was, *"How can man be born again when he is old? He cannot enter a second time into his mother's womb and be born, can he?"* (v. 4). Without hesitation, Jesus explained this rebirth is not in the physical sense. Instead, it's a spiritual rebirth *"of the water and the Spirit"* (v. 5). This rebirth is spoken of in different terms with a like meaning in 2 Corinthians 5:17, when the apostle Paul wrote, *"Therefore if anyone is in Christ, he is a new creature; the old things passed away; behold, new things have come."*

In two separate passages in chapter 1, Peter uses the phrase *"born again"* to emphasize the transformation before becoming a Christian compared to after obeying the Gospel. It is of great interest to note that this spiritual rebirth is what God causes to happen (v. 3) instead of what man causes. Just as a mother endures the pain and makes the effort in a physical birth, God is the one who does the work in this spiritual rebirth. When a person obeys the Gospel (1 Peter 4:17) in confession, repentance, and baptism for the remission of sins, he waves the white flag of surrender. However, it is God who, in His infinite wisdom and mercy before the foundation of the world (1 Peter 1:20), made provision for His enemies to lay down their weapons and be transformed to become His children. It's only through this rebirth, this being born again, that we have a hope that is alive and certain, being founded on the promise that—like Christ—even if we are put to death because of our faith in God, we too will be resurrected from death to eternal life.

 ## 2. WE ARE PROTECTED BY THE POWER OF GOD THROUGH FAITH

In waving the white flag of surrender as enemy combatants, we enter an extraordinary relationship with God. The apostle Paul explained this strong relationship when he writes the church in Ephesus and describes those who once were *"separate from Christ, excluded from the commonwealth of Israel, and strangers to the covenants of promise, having no hope and without God in the world"* (Eph.2:12).However,that's not where their story ends. That may be who they used to be as those outside of the covenant with God. Still, Paul continued with a sweet statement, *"But now in Christ Jesus you*

who formerly were far off have been brought near by the blood of Christ" (Eph. 2:13). He further emphasized that they are no longer strangers to the covenant of God. Instead, they are fellow citizens with the saints and are of God's household (Eph. 2:19).

This new covenant is not cheap and is signed and secured on God's side with the blood of His Son Jesus. On our side, we continually hold fast to Jesus in faith (1 Pet. 1:5). It is through our continual reliance upon God through Jesus that the promise of God remains. If the promise of salvation is going to elude us, it will not be because God has changed. It will solely be our fault if we abandoned our surrender. However, as faithful followers of Jesus, you and I have the assurance of the power of God to protect our salvation. That should give you and me peace as we face the uncertainties of the future.

 3. WE WILL RECEIVE AN INHERITANCE AS PART OF GOD'S FAMILY

As the transformation has occurred and the enemy has become the redeemed child, there is a promise of a tremendous inheritance that Peter wants to serve as an inspiration for the Christians to whom he is writing. Considering the difficult trials and struggles they are enduring (1 Pet. 1:6) and will continue to endure, he reminds them of the temporary nature of such and emphasizes the eternal nature of their reward in Christ Jesus. He describes this inheritance as "*imperishable and undefiled and will not fade away, reserved in heaven for you*" (1 Pet. 1:4). This untarnished and unstrained inheritance is secure for those who hold fast to the faith in the face of an unrelenting and intense fire. Peter stresses that faithfulness through this proofing (burning off the dross in refinement of one's faith) will also *"result in praise, and glory, and honor at the revelation of Jesus Christ"* (1 Pet. 1:7). This praise, glory, and honor are going to be poured out on us by God when the inheritance is fully realized, at the revelation of Jesus Christ.

★ WRAP-UP ⟫⟫ SURRENDER TO HIS GOSPEL

I'm glad my son and I had the opportunity to discuss being a disciple of Jesus because it caused me to stop consider the incompleteness of the statement "giving God our best." I guess I had just always taken for granted that we were never going to be perfect in our discipleship, so our best was really all we could give. However, that's only part of the truth. God has never told us throughout Scripture that He wants our very best. He has always desired our total and complete surrender in submission. He wants you and me to decide to quit fighting against Him. He longs for us to wave the white flag of surrender, so we can receive the blessing He wants to bestow upon us. However, that can only happen when we cease being enemy combatants and accept the grace He extends to us through the preaching of the Gospel of His Son, Jesus Christ.

> **HE HAS ALWAYS DESIRED OUR TOTAL AND COMPLETE SURRENDER IN SUBMISSION.**

FIELD NOTES » SURRENDER TO HIS GOSPEL

1. Why do you think the phrase "We just have to give God our best" has become so ingrained in many Christians? If you believe this phrase has some validity to it, why? If you think this phrase is limited or lacking, in what ways is it lacking, and why would you conclude such?

2. When you hear or read the word "Surrender," what comes to your mind? What would it take for a soldier to get to the point where surrender was the best avenue to take? What would happen inside that soldier as he processes his thoughts and finally surrenders?

3. What is an enemy combatant, and why do you believe the author describes the enemies of God in such a way? In your own life, think about how you lived before becoming a disciple of Jesus Christ. If you've yet to surrender to the Gospel, how does it strike you to hear you are an enemy combatant of God?

4. Of all the descriptions of the Gospel found in this chapter, which one or two points is most precious to you? Why are these the ones that hit home in your life?

5. Why do you believe it's essential to keep the reward of heaven in front of the mind of a Christian? In 1 Peter chapter 1, Peter wants the disciples never to forget where they are going. Why do you think this is significant? How has this been helpful in your life as you encounter the fires of proofing?

"HAVE YOU EVER REALIZED THAT YOU CAN GIVE THINGS TO GOD THAT ARE OF VALUE TO HIM? OR ARE YOU JUST SITTING AROUND DAYDREAMING ABOUT THE GREATNESS OF HIS REDEMPTION WHILE NEGLECTING ALL THE THINGS YOU COULD BE DOING FOR HIM? I'M NOT REFERRING TO WORKS WHICH COULD BE REGARDED AS DIVINE AND MIRACULOUS, BUT ORDINARY, SIMPLE HUMAN THINGS—THINGS WHICH WOULD BE EVIDENCE TO GOD THAT YOU ARE TOTALLY SURRENDERED TO HIM."

- OSWALD CHAMBERS[1]

BRIEFING — SURRENDER TO HIS PURPOSE

After a three-week siege, on October 19, 1781, the British army under the command of Lieutenant General Charles Cornwallis officially agreed to the complete surrender to the combined French American forces at Yorktown, Virginia. Prior to this, with 7,500 soldiers, Cornwallis, under the command of General Henry Clinton (1730–1795), moved to the Virginia peninsula with the intent to fortify a port as a base for naval operations.

In response, the American Continental army under the command of General George Washington and the French army under the command of Lieutenant General Rochambeau marched their combined troops numbering over 17,000 to Yorktown. Along with this effort, the French feet comprised of 24 ships, under the command of Admiral de Grasse, was positioned along the Chesapeake, preventing the British navy from assisting Cornwallis in Yorktown. The siege worked.

Realizing his inevitable and dire circumstances, Lord Cornwallis decided to surrender, only he never attended the surrendering ceremony himself. Instead, after having been denied his request for a typical British ceremony of this nature by General George Washington in response to what had happened months early to American General Lincoln, history records that Cornwallis sent his second in command General O'Hara to deliver his own sword as a sign of surrender.

Dr. James Thatcher, a Massachusetts physician who served in the Continental Army, preserved this historical event in his diary entitled *A Military Journal During the American Revolutionary War, from 1775 to 1783*. I include this lengthy entry because it paints the picture of this day more effectively than any retelling of historical facts could possibly accomplish.

> At about twelve o'clock, the combined army was arranged and drawn up in two lines extending more than a mile in length. Te Americans were drawn up in a line on the right side of the road, and the French occupied the left. At the head of the former the great American commander, mounted on his noble courser, took his station, attended by his aides. At the head of the latter was posted the excellent Count Rochambeau and his suite. Te French troops, in complete uniform, displayed a martial and noble appearance, their band of music, of which the timbrel formed a part, is a delightful novelty, and produced while marching to the ground a most enchanting effect. Te Americans, though not all in uniform nor their dress so neat, yet exhibited an erect soldierly air, and every countenance beamed with satisfaction and joy. The concourse of spectators from the country was prodigious, in point of numbers probably equal to the military, but universal silence and order prevailed.
>
> It was about two o'clock when the captive army advanced through the line formed for their reception. Every eye was prepared to gaze on Lord Cornwallis, the object of peculiar interest and solicitude; but he disappointed our anxious expectations; pretending indisposition, he made General O'Hara his substitute as the leader

of his army. This officer was followed by the conquered troops in a slow and solemn step, with shouldered arms, colors cased, and drums beating a British march. Having arrived at the head of the line, General O'Hara, elegantly mounted, advanced to his excellency, the commander-in-chief, taking of his hat, and apologized for the non-appearance of Earl Cornwallis. With his usual dignity and politeness his excellency pointed to Major General Lincoln for directions, by whom the British army was conducted into a spacious field where it was intended they should ground their arms.

The royal troops, while marching through the line formed by the allied army, exhibited a decent and neat appearance, as respects arms and clothing, for their commander opened his store and directed every soldier to be furnished with a new suit complete, prior to the capitulation. But in their line of march we remarked a disorderly and un-soldierly conduct; their step was irregular and their ranks frequently broken.

But it was in the field when they came to the last act of the drama, that the spirit and pride of the British soldier was put to the severest test—here their mortification could not be concealed. Some of the platoon oficers appeared to be exceedingly chagrined when giving the word "ground arms", and I am a witness that they performed this duty in a very un-oficer-like manner, and that many of the soldiers manifested a sullen temper, throwing their arms on the pile with violence, as if determined to render them useless. This irregularity, however, was checked by the authority of General Lincoln. After having grounded their arms and divested themselves of their accouterments, the captive troops were conducted back to

Yorktown and guarded by our troops until they could be removed to the place of their destination.

The British troops that were stationed at Gloucester surrendered at the same time, and in the same manner to the command of the Duke de Lauzun.

This must be a very interesting and gratifying transaction to General Lincoln, who having himself been obliged to surrender an army to a haughty foe the last year, has now assigned him the pleasing duty of giving laws to a conquered army in return, and of reflecting that the terms which were imposed on him are adopted as a basis of the surrender in the present instance. It is a very gratifying circumstance that every degree of harmony, confidence, and friendly intercourse subsisted between the American and French troops during the campaign, no contest except an emulous spirit to excel in exploits and enterprise against the common enemy, and a desire to be celebrated in the annals of history for an ardent love of great and heroic actions.

We are not to be surprised that the pride of the British officers is humbled on this occasion, as they have always entertained an exalted opinion of their own military prowess, and affected to view the Americans as a contemptible, undisciplined rabble. But there is no display of magnanimity when a great commander shrinks from the inevitable misfortunes of war, and when it is considered that Lord Cornwallis has frequently appeared in splendid triumph at the head of his army by which he is almost adored, we conceive it incumbent on him cheerfully to participate in their misfortunes and degradations, however humiliating; but it is said he gives himself up entirely to vexation and despair.[2]

Those are the historical facts; however, what happened during the surrender draws us to understand better that the one surrendering doesn't get to set the terms. They are not in a position of power or strength, and pride should not be a part of the equation for any surrendering party. All they can do is merely agree to the terms of the victor. Unlike the British troops and officers, we must not begrudgingly lay our weapons down at our surrender through submission to the purpose of God. Pride, even when accompanied by actions of surrender is damnable. There is no place for it. That's why Jesus said that if anyone wants to come after Him, he must *"deny himself, take up his cross and follow"* (Matt. 16:24). In other words, there is a complete surrender, or there is no surrender at all. Pride is laid down, and a new purpose is assumed. That is, we take up the purpose of God for our lives in both our words and our walk.

But what is His purpose?

INTEL >>> SURRENDER TO HIS PURPOSE

As we begin in this section, it would do us well to remember that we serve a God of purpose. He doesn't go about randomly or carelessly. He is the long-term strategic planner of the universe, and His purpose reaches from eternity past to eternity future. He thinks of everything and knows what we need, even before the foundation of the world was laid (Eph. 1:4; 1 Pet. 1:20). He is not short-sighted like we are at times. Instead, His purpose encompasses not only the ultimate end of all His creation but His desired end for all mankind—salvation. Without hesitation nor uncertainty, He asserts through the prophet Isaiah in chapter 46, verses 9 and 10,

> *Remember the former things long past,*
> *For I am God, and there is no other;*
> *I am God, and there is no one like Me,*
> *Declaring the end from the beginning,*
> *And from ancient times things which have not been done,*
> *Saying, "My purpose will be established,*
> *And I will accomplish all My good pleasure."*

The apostle Paul, when speaking with the elders from Ephesus, makes a statement that draws us closer to understanding the whole purpose of God when he says, *"For I did not shrink from declaring to you the whole purpose of God"* (Acts 20:27). Upon further investigation into the text, Paul claims to have declared to them what was "profitable" (v. 20), the necessity for both Jews and Gentiles of *"repentance toward God and faith in our Lord Jesus Christ"* (v. 21), the *"gospel of the grace of God"* (v. 24), and of "the kingdom" (v. 25). In short, by inspiration of the Holy Spirit, Paul claims to have not withheld any aspect of the purpose of God for mankind.

With God's ultimate purpose for mankind being clearly identified, our salvation, we also know that because mankind has free will, we can choose whether we will be submissive and surrender to His purpose. While God is always faithful, we have the option of whether we will be in return. In Luke 7:30, we read of a case just like this when Luke says a group of Pharisees and lawyers have *"rejected God's purpose for themselves, not having been baptized by John."* So, it would do us well to see from chapter one the Christians to whom Peter is writing have surrendered to the Gospel of Jesus Christ; however, now they must understand the depth of such a surrender and choose to completely give their lives over to the purpose of God in this life and not merely sit around and wait on their eternal reward. That's the same choice you and I must make today as we consider surrendering to God in our words and walk.

 ## SURRENDER TO THE PURPOSE OF GOD IN OUR WORDS

There is great power in words. In a culture inundated with social media, we regularly see posts that relay news stories and attempt to persuade opinions. We observe rants and apologies, along with special announcements and advertisements. "Clickbait" and satiric headlines over promise and often under-deliver. Emotions are stirred, and timeouts are given. It is genuinely an interesting study of the power of words. Psychologists have conducted studies and interviews and observed that words have the power to 1) transmit and exchange information, 2) influence and control the behavior of others, 3) establish and demonstrate social cohesion, and 4) imagine and create new ways of experiencing life.[3] This is probably not surprising to any of us because our own lives and interactions with people affirm these conclusions. We know what it feels like to have people speak to us using harsh and kind words, and we experienced shared ideas that shaped and perhaps changed the direction of our lives. If you're a parent, you've regularly used words to help shape your children's view of life and learning, people and politics, and most importantly, sin and salvation. Throughout God's Word, we also read and learn of the power of words. Consider the following passages that demonstrate the positive and negative effects of our words.

- **Psalm 35:20**—*"For they do not speak peace, But they devise deceitful words against those who are quiet in the land."*
- **Psalm 55:21**—*"His speech was smoother than butter, But his heart was war; His words were softer than oil, Yet they were drawn swords."*
- **Psalm 59:12**—*"On account of the sin of their mouth and the words of their lips, Let them even be caught in their pride, And on account of curses and lies which they utter."*
- **Proverbs 7:5**—*"That they may keep you from an adulteress, From the foreigner who flatters with her words."*
- **Proverbs 12:25**—*"Anxiety in a man's heart weighs it down, But a good word makes it glad."*
- **Proverbs 15:23**—*"A man has joy in an apt answer, And how delightful is a timely word!"*

Why does God want those who have surrendered in submission to the Gospel to use their words for His purpose? Ultimately, our identity changes once the decision has been made to follow Jesus. Like the apostle Paul we consider ourselves *"crucified with Christ,"* no longer living for ourselves but living *"by faith in the Son of God"* (Gal. 2:20). With this complete change, including the heart, soul, body, and mind (Matt. 22:37), it stands to reason the words we speak would also be changed.

That's what Peter is addressing in 1 Peter 2. Since they have tasted the kindness of God (v. 3), they are to continually strive for growth with respect to their salvation. They are continually learning and implementing the truths found in God's Word into their lives. It's no longer a religion they practice, and it is no longer about their heritage, either Jew or Greek. It's about a life change; they are to long for the Word of God as a newborn baby longs for milk.

As we consider our own lives in light of this expectation and change in desire, we are challenged to ask ourselves if the impact of our salvation is enough to drive us in this manner. The price for our redemption was not cheap (1 Pet. 1:18-19). If we ever lose sight of that, if this fact ceases to impact our hearts and minds significantly, we will fade in our devotion. Only when we remain on fire for the Lord because of what He has done for us do we want to do His will with our words. That's why Peter reminds these Christians in 1 Peter 2:3 that they have tasted the kindness of the Lord, so live as if that is the case.

Specifically, Peter reminds them of their new identity in chapter 2, verse 9, when he writes, *"But you are a chosen race, a royal priesthood, a holy nation, a people for God's own possession...."* When you and I surrendered to the Gospel, we stopped being our own. Sure, we can always rebel and leave God behind; however, the only way we will be pleasing and remain under His protection for eternity (1 Pet. 1:5) is to remain His *"possession."* That word denotes "a people for an acquisition {or purchase}; means a people acquired or purchased to Himself in a peculiar or unique manner."[4] That's precisely what He did for those who obey the Gospel through the blood of Jesus.

When we accept and take our new identity to heart—the place a true transformation occurs—our words will reflect this surrender through submission. That's exactly what Peter says next. You are a people for God's own possession, *"so that you may proclaim the excellencies of Him who has called you out of darkness into His marvelous light"* (1 Pet. 2:9). There are many keywords that are focus-worthy; however, for our section of interest, consider the word *"proclaim."* In Greek, it means "to declare abroad, make widely known."[5] It automatically brings with it a demand and expectation that, as Christians, we will use our words to declare to the "excellencies of God" "the superiority of God revealed in the work of salvation."[6] You have an amazing and wonderful story to tell as a child of God. Our identity changed when we laid down our weapons as enemy combatants and fully surrendered by submitting to the Gospel. We went from being in darkness to being in His marvelous light. You and I now have a living hope (1 Pet. 1:3), born through the living and enduring Word of God (1 Pet. 1:23), guaranteed by the resurrection of the living stone that has been rejected by so many throughout time (1 Pet. 2:4).

Don't ever forget with your transformation comes the responsibility of a proclamation. We must tell His story and the impact of the death, burial, and resurrection of Jesus Christ in our personal lives. To refuse to do so or to hide behind our insecurities is to trust in ourselves more than we trust in God. Moses tried to get out of going to Pharaoh, and God did not stand for it (Exodus 4). Instead, the text says that God responded to Moses' excuse of not being eloquent in speech by saying, *"Who has made man's mouth? Or who makes him mute or deaf, or seeing or blind? Is it not I, the Lord? Now then, go and I, even I, will be with your mouth, and teach you what you are to say"* (4:11- 12). God has given you the words to speak in His Word. You surrendered for a reason. Tell people why. That's His purpose for your words.

 # SURRENDER TO THE PURPOSE OF GOD IN OUR WALK

You have most likely heard that people watch what you do more than they listen to what you say. Whether or not this is true, I don't know because research is difficult to quantify; however, I do know the apostle Paul had to address a group of Jews who were caught in the trap of saying one thing and doing another, and the consequences were grave. In Romans 2, after having told the Gentiles they are without excuse before God in chapter 1, he asserts the Jews are also without excuse (2:1). This must have been received as a shock to the original audience because the Jews were saying the right things. From what we can learn from this text, they were even teaching the Gentiles to do right according to the Law of Moses; however, the lack of observance on their part of their own words is why Paul writes, *"You who boast in the Law, through your breaking the Law, do you dishonor God? For the 'Name of God is blasphemed among the Gentiles because of you,' just as it is written"* (2:23-24). Inconsistency leads to confusion, and in this case, the consequence was even more significant—the very name of God is blasphemed—to "smite with reports or words, speak evil of, slander, rail."[7] All because of the hypocritical walk of those who claim to be His covenant people.

On the positive side, we also read and learn of individuals like Hananiah, Mishael, and Azariah, who lived boldly, unapologetically, and consistently for the Lord in the face of horrific dangers. In Daniel 3, we read of one occasion when Hananiah, Mishael, and Azariah (more commonly known by their Babylonian names Shadrach, Meshach, and Abed-nego) were amongst the crowd told to bow down to the golden image commissioned by the Babylonian king Nebuchadnezzar. Refusing to do so, they understood there could be grave consequences; however, the decision was already made as to whose they were before this option to bow down presented itself. Therefore, when threatened with the fiery furnace, they replied to Nebuchadnezzar.

> *O Nebuchadnezzar, we do not need to give you an answer concerning this matter. If it be so, our God whom we serve is able to deliver us from the furnace of blazing fire; and He will deliver us out of your hand, O king. But even if He does not, let it be known to you, O king, that we are not going to serve your gods or worship the golden image that you have set up. (Daniel 3:16-18)*

Most likely, you know the rest of the account. They were thrown into a furnace so hot that those who threw them in died in the process. However, the three bold followers of God did not perish because the power of God protected them. There are more details to this account, but it's the statement made by Nebuchadnezzar after there was not even a hair on the heads of the three men singed that needs to be emphasized.

> *Blessed be the God of Shadrach, Meshach and Abed-nego, who has sent His angel and delivered His servants who put their trust in Him, violating the king's command, and yielded up their bodies so as not to serve or worship any god except their own God. Therefore, I make a decree that any people, nation or tongue that speaks anything offensive against the God of Shadrach, Meshach and Abed-nego shall be torn limb from limb and their houses reduced to a rubbish heap, inasmuch as there is no other god who is able to deliver in this way. (Daniel 3:28-29.*

What are the valuable lessons for you and me to learn? First, don't wait for the music to begin playing to make up our minds about whose side we are on. Determine beforehand what our response will be when situations arise. That way, we aren't hurriedly scurrying to process the circumstances in the heat of the moment. Second, our confidence in God can't only be in the future. We must have confidence in Him now. He can do wonderful things in and through our lives; however, if He chooses not to respond in the way we desire, we will still trust Him. Lastly, our convictions lived out for others to see do have the potential to bring others to recognize and glorify God.

That's the challenge we find in 1 Peter 2 as we consider surrendering to the purpose of God in our walk. In this text, Peter commands the Christians to *"abstain from fleshly lust"* (v. 11), *"keep your behavior excellent among the Gentiles"* (v. 12), and *"submit yourselves for the Lord's sake to every human institution"* (v. 13). It's the reasons behind these instructions that we need to focus on if we are going to understand the acts themselves.

- (v. 11)— *"Abstain from fleshly lusts."*
    - Why? They *"wage war against the soul."*
- (v. 12)—*"Keep your behavior excellent among the Gentiles"*
    - Why? *"So that in the thing in which they slander you as evildoers, they may because of your good deeds as they observe them, glorify God in the day of visitation."*
- (v.13)—*Submit yourselves for the Lord's sake to every human institution"*
    - Why? *"For such is the will of God that by doing right you may silence the ignorance of foolish men"*

The benefits are really two-fold but melded together into one purpose. There's a benefit for us in that our moral character, our inner being, is not caught up in the corruption that comes with living an unrestrained life according to the flesh. However, the ultimate purpose we abstain from fleshly lusts is wrapped into the same reason we are to keep our behavior excellent amongst those who do not know God, so they can observe our good deeds as we live consistently with what we proclaim. This will draw them to glorify God in the day of visitation. However, the opposite is also true. If we do not surrender in our walk to God's purpose and claim to be God's redeemed children, we may keep those from glorifying God on the day of visitation.

WRAP-UP » SURRENDER TO HIS PURPOSE

On October 17, 1781, General Cornwallis had a letter delivered to George Washington in which he laid out his request to surrender the British army at Yorktown.

> *York in Virginia 17th October 1781 1/2 past 4 P.M.*
> *Sir*
> *I have this moment been honoured with your Excellency's letter dated this day. The time limited for sending my answer will not admit of entering into the detail of Articles, but the basis of my proposals will be that the Garrisons of York and Gloucester shall be prisoners of War with the Customary honours, And for the convenience of the individuals which I have the honour to Command, that the British shall be sent to Britain, and the Germans to Germany, under the engagement not to serve against France, America or their Allies untill released or regularly exchanged. Tat all Arms and publick Stores shall be delivered up to you, but that the usual indulgence*

of side Arms to officers and of retaining private property shall be granted to Officers & Soldiers, and that the interests of several individuals in Civil Capacities & connected with us, shall be attended to. If Your Excellency thinks that a continuance of the suspension of hostilities will be necessary to transmit your Answer I shall have no objections to the hour that you propose. I have the honor to be Sir Your most obedient & most humble Servant Cornwallis[8]

While Cornwallis admitted to many concessions of surrender, he also maintained a sense that he was in a position to make demands of the conquering army. Similarly, when we surrender in submission to the purpose of God, when we obey the Gospel, we aren't in a position to say what we will and will not do; otherwise, we are not telling God we surrender. We are merely asking for a cease-fre. A cease-fre will not save. Only a total and complete surrender will do. That means even submitting in how we intentionally use our words and the purpose of our walk. When we surrender, we accept whatever difficulties may arise. God is faithful to His promises and tells us about a future glory that will be ours in eternity when Jesus returns; however, that doesn't mean we will not suffer the difficulties being a follower of God may bring in this life from those who continue to be enemy combatants as we once were. We must bear up under such suffering, just as Christ did for us. As Peter explains to the Christians in our text,

For you have been called for this purpose, since Christ also suffered for you, leaving you an example for you to follow in His steps, who committed no sin, nor was any deceit found in His mouth; and while being reviled, He did not revile in return; while suffering, He uttered no threats, but kept entrusting Himself to Him who judges righteously; and He Himself bore our sins in His body on the cross, so that we might die to sin and live to righteousness; for by His wounds you were healed. (1 Peter 2:21-24)

FIELD NOTES » SURRENDER TO HIS PURPOSE

1. In your life, have you ever struggled with pride when it comes to surrendering to God in any way? If so, in what ways?

2. In considering the strategic plan of God to accomplish His purpose of the redemption of mankind, what can we conclude about Him? His nature? His fortitude? His determination? His view of mankind? What can we learn about God when considering His purpose of redemption?

3. In what ways have your words brought to light the purpose of God? In what ways have your words hidden in the shadows the purpose of God?

4. Why do you think most struggle to allow their words to reflect their surrender to God's purpose? Why do we struggle to discuss God's purpose with our friends, co-workers, and even family members when we aren't afraid to discuss so many other topics? How are you using your words to advance the purpose of God?

5. In what ways do you believe God can use our walk in this life to accomplish His purpose of the redemption of mankind? In what ways can our walk hinder that purpose? How are you doing in your walk currently?

"THE FULL ACTING OUT OF THE SELF'S SURRENDER TO GOD THEREFORE DEMANDS PAIN: THIS ACTION, TO BE PERFECT, MUST BE DONE FROM THE PURE WILL TO OBEY, IN THE ABSENCE, OR IN THE TEETH, OF INCLINATION."

- C.S. LEWIS[1]

SURRENDER TO HIS PURSUITS

If you hear the name Martin James Monti, does it mean anything to you? Monti was born in St. Louis, Missouri, on October 24, 1921, and was one of seven children. Of the seven, four of his brothers went on to serve in the United States military, so one could say he had a home life that taught him to take pride in America and stand up for her. However, his home wasn't the only influence in his life. A Canadian-American Roman Catholic priest by the name of Charles Edward Coughlin, who ran a very popular radio program from Detroit, Michigan, was also a significant voice in the mind of Monti and would prove to be a major driving force in the direction Monti would take.

Coughlin was like many modern-day television evangelists, only his stage was the radio. By 1934, history records that he had amassed a following estimated to have been in the tens of millions throughout Canada and America. Monti was one of those followers, and he listened, soaking up Coughlin's worldview as much as possible. Initially, Coughlin supported then President Franklin Delano Roosevelt; however, over the years, he developed a great dislike for The New Deal and thus departed from his support of FDR. He began to see these new liberal socialist programs in view of an overall greater problem: communism. However, in his journey to anti-communism, he would also abandon all support for capitalism and became anti-Semitic in the process. In 1936, the Catholic Church tried to silence this very outspoken and well-known priest; however, that only made him more powerful and influential amongst his followers. Finally, as WWII broke out in 1939, his broadcasts were forced off the air, but the effect of his messages had already corrupted the mind of Martin James Monti. Coughlin's pro-Fascist views and sympathies for Germany and Italy had infiltrated and changed this 21-year-old from Missouri so much so that in October of 1942, Monti visited Coughlin just before the young man joined the U.S. Airforce.

Having come from a family where so many of his brothers decided to join the U.S. in the fight, Monti's endeavor should not have been a great surprise; however, what Monti did after reaching the rank of first lieutenant and while stationed at the Pomigliano Airfield in southern Italy with the 354th Air Service Squadron remains a great shock in military history. Having qualified during his training to fly the P-38, Monti seized the opportunity to volunteer to test a refurbished P-38 at the base. The soldiers and mechanics were unaware and thought nothing of it, and Monti was approved for the test flight. While in the air, he made his way to northern Italy and landed at a German-occupied location on October 13. Initially, unconvinced by his claims of defection, Monti would be counted as a POW and placed in an internment camp; however, he was persistent and consistent in his claim. His anti-capitalist, anti-communist, and anti-Semitic views grew in volume to the point where he was eventually taken out of the POW camp and allowed to wear the uniform of the Third Reich, being used through propaganda arms of the German military.

Eventually, as the Allied forces continued to gain ground in the various offensives of the war, Monti surrendered to the U.S. military on May 10, 1945 and was tried for treason. During his time as a prisoner in American custody, Monti explained that he defected to the Germans not because he was anti-American but because he was pro-American. He believed America misidentified the real enemy—

Russia—and he had to fight against Bolshevism because, in his mind, it posed the greatest threat to America. Through numerous appeals and one deal he made with the U.S. military, Monti would remain in prison until 1960 when he was granted parole.[2]

We begin chapter three with the account of Martin James Monti because it addresses, albeit in a non-patriotic manner, the subject of an enemy combatant becoming a soldier for the side he was initially fighting against. In military terms, treason is a very taboo and negative subject, so much so that in the history of America, this charge has been used so few times and even prosecuted much less, one could say it's just a law on paper that is meant to deter flipping and fighting against one's homeland. However, spiritually, treason happens so regularly that it is challenging to discuss surrender to the pursuits of God without exploring what it means to turn against the side on which you began the battle. Let me explain.

> **SPIRITUALLY, TREASON HAPPENS SO REGULARLY.**

The apostle Paul was known as Saul at one time. He was so dedicated to his heritage and upbringing that he described himself *"as to the Law, a Pharisee; as to zeal, a persecutor of the church; as to the righteousness which is in the Law, found blameless"* (Phil. 3:5-6). He spoke of his former aggression toward the church of God in 1 Corinthians 15:9 and Galatians 1:13. Saul was not a man who sat on the bench and was passive toward early Christianity. Instead, he was violent and aggressive and intended to erase the movement known as The Way (Acts 8:1-3; 9:1-2), but everything changed for

Saul one day. Not only did his name change, but his allegiance also changed in that instead of fighting against the advancement of Jesus Christ, he devoted his life to spreading the message of the living hope in Jesus. In reality, he started as an enemy combatant but changed to be one of the mighty warriors for the sake of Christ.

The apostle Paul stands as a perfect example when we surrender in submission to the Gospel of Jesus Christ and buy into the purpose of God. Eventually, we must decide to pick up the weapons of the Lord and go to battle on His behalf. I want us to consider this changing of sides in this lesson. Before someone who was once an enemy of God picks up the weapons and arms himself to fight for God, he must be convicted that God's side is worth the fight.

INTEL ›› SURRENDER TO HIS PURSUITS

As we turn our attention to 1 Peter 3, this is the thought as we consider surrendering to God's pursuits. In the previous chapter, we discussed His purpose, our salvation. Chapter 3, similarly, carries through the significant theme of submission. As we saw in chapter 2 regarding submitting to governments and in the servant/master relationship, in chapter 3 we see submission brought into the marriage relationship. As students of the Bible who desire a more profound understanding, we should ask ourselves why our submission in marriage impacts the pursuits of God and how does our approach to suffering accomplish the pursuits of God?

 PURSUITS OF GOD IN MARRIAGE

Marriage is a great blessing given to mankind by God. When we stop to think of the establishments that come from God instead of from man's creative works, we see that the concept of government is God's plan for keeping order and dealing with those who do evil in this life (Rom. 13). Before the foundation of the world, another establishment—the church—was crafted into the plan of God. Those redeemed through the blood of Jesus would be the pillar and support of the truth (1 Tim. 3:15) and would help one another grow in spiritual maturity as God intends (Eph. 4:11-13). Marriage is the first establishment or entity that originated with God (Gen. 2:22-24). The purpose of marriage included the bearing of fruit or offspring; however, if that's all we understand the purpose of marriage to be, we are cutting short the beauty and depth of which this great institution is worthy. Plus, we aren't doing ourselves any favors because what we understand the purpose of marriage to be will impact our approach to our marriages.

In Marriage, God Pursues the Well-being of the Home

"In the same way, you wives be submissive to your own husbands..." (1 Pet. 3:1).
"You husbands in the same way, live with your wives in an understanding way..." (1 Pet. 3:7).

The structure keeps the physical house solid and able to withstand the stresses placed upon it by the wind and rain cast against it.

When the structure is secure, those inside the house are safe. If at any time shortcuts were taken in the building of the home, they will often be revealed in the most stressful times. Unfortunately, by the time they show, it's often too late, and destruction occurs.

Spiritually speaking, it's the same. When the structure is firm and secure as God intends, those in the home will be blessed. That is why the psalmist wrote in Psalm 127:1, *"Unless the Lord builds the house, They labor in vain who build it; Unless the Lord guards the city, The watchman keeps awake in vain."* With this warning also comes the promise that when God is the builder and the watchman, our house is not built in a futile manner. That's why marriage and the creative order revealed in Biblical marriage are pivotal to the spiritual well-being of those in the family.

In Genesis 2:22-24, God, through the pen of Moses, declares the beginning of this structure when He writes,

> *The Lord God fashioned into a woman the rib which He had taken from the man, and brought her to the man. The man said,*
>
> > *"This is now bone of my bones,*
> > *And flesh of my flesh;*
> > *She shall be called Woman,*
> > *Because she was taken out of Man."*
>
> *For this reason a man shall leave his father and his mother, and be joined to his wife; and they shall become one flesh.*

Paul appeals to this same creative order in 1 Corinthians 11:3 when he writes, *"But I want you to understand that Christ is the head of every man, and the man is the head of a woman, and God is the head of Christ."* The question that lingers is, why would he do this? Why would Jesus appeal to the creative order in Matthew 19 when answering the questions regarding divorce? It's because this creative order, which is not inconsequential, is foundational to God's intent for the home. It's here we find that God, in His infinite wisdom, instituted marriage to bring both blessing and functionality to the family.

Thus, when Peter in 1 Peter 3:1 instructs wives to be submissive to their own husbands and in 1 Peter 3:7 instructs husbands *"In the same way live with your wives in an understanding way,"* he is telling them that their relationship is a statement of their surrender through submission to God. Husbands should not look down on their wives and treat them as less. They are not! In fact, Peter drives this point home to these Christian men when he writes, *"Show her honor as a fellow heir of the grace of life, so that your prayers will not be hindered"* (1 Pet. 3:7). So, on the one hand, we see wives voluntarily placing themselves under the authority of their husbands, yet on the other, husbands are honoring their wives. On both occasions, it takes complete and total surrender to the pursuits of God for marriage. Husbands then spiritually lead, provide, and protect as God intends. Wives love their husbands and children, making the home a place where physical and spiritual maturity occurs in peace and support.

In Marriage, God Pursues the Souls of People

When Peter instructs wives in 1 Peter 3:1 to be submissive to their own husbands, he calls wives to show great strength and devotion to God. This submission is a free-will, voluntary, self-disciplined placing of herself beneath her husband in authority. In doing so, she demonstrates complete surrender to the pursuits of God in marriage and displays her connectedness with the pursuits of God. Peter brought this out when he writes in verses 1-2, *"...So that even if any of them are disobedient to the word, **they may be won** without a word by the behavior of their wives, as they observe your chaste and respectful behavior"* (emp. added). As we've already established in the previous chapter, God's purpose for mankind is salvation. He demonstrates that in His unending love and patience, constantly receiving those to Himself who lay their weapons down as enemy combatants and surrender through submission to the Gospel. Interestingly, this pursuit of God is why a wife submits to her husband in this text. When a wife is convicted that the pursuit of God for the soul of her husband is central to their marriage, she responds in a manner that shows she is concerned about that which concerns God. Her submissiveness demonstrates this.

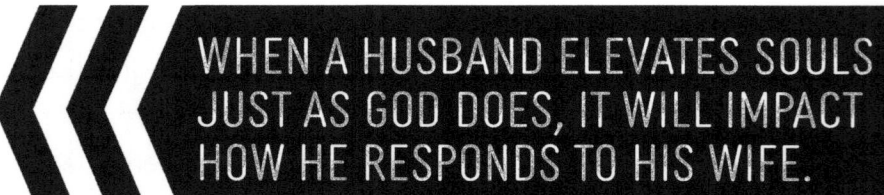

WHEN A HUSBAND ELEVATES SOULS JUST AS GOD DOES, IT WILL IMPACT HOW HE RESPONDS TO HIS WIFE.

In the same way, Peter wrote in 1 Peter 3:7 that husbands are to "***in the same way,*** *live with your wives in an understanding way...*" (emp. added) because of the exact same reason why a wife is instructed to demonstrate self-discipline in submitting to her husband. He is to respond to God in faithfulness, pursuing the same thing God desires—the soul of his wife. When a husband elevates souls just as God does, it will impact how he responds to his wife. His living with her in an understanding way, knowing he could dominate her physically because she's someone who is physically weaker but choosing not to do so, requires the same as the submitting wife—free-willing, with a voluntary attitude, and with the backbone of self-discipline.

In verse 8, Peter emphasizes the essential qualities required for both husbands and wives, which are necessary to accomplish the pursuits of God in their marriage. These same qualities are vital in the spirit of the one who is to submit to authorities of a civil nature and, in context, servants to their masters.

> *To sum up, all of you be **harmonious, sympathetic, brotherly, kindhearted,** and **humble in spirit;** not returning evil for evil or insult for insult, but giving a blessing instead; for you were called for the very purpose that you might inherit a blessing* (emp. added).

It does us well to consider these traits in a more in-depth manner.

- **Harmonious**—ὁμόφρων, *homóphrōn*; A combination of *homós*, "one and the same," and *phren*, "mind, understanding"; of the same mind, like-minded.[3]
- **Sympathetic**— συμπαθής, *sumpathés*; A combination of *sún*, "together or with," and *páthos*, "suffering, misfortune"; compassionate, sympathizing.[4]
- **Brotherly**— Φιλάδελφος, *philádelphos*: A combination of *phílos*, "friend," and *adelphós*, "brother"; loving one's brother, brotherly affectionate.[5]

- **Kindhearted**— εὔσπλαγχνος, *eúsplagchnos:* A combination of *eú,* "well," and *splágchnon,* "bowel"; tender-hearted, full of compassion, pity.⁶
- **Humble in Spirit**— ταπεινόφρων, *tapeinóphrōn:* A word that means "low," "lowly," or "serville," usually with the disparaging sense of obsequiousness or submissiveness.⁷

 ## PURSUITS OF GOD IN SUFFERING

When we investigate the book of 1 Peter, the word *suffering* stands out like a bright light as one of, if not the primary emphasis in the book. Being found 17 times, third most behind God (39 times) and Christ (23 times), *suffering* is both readily on the minds of these Christians and the apostle Peter, as much is written about the expectation disciples of Jesus have regarding suffering and the intimate connection to Christ and His suffering this accomplishes.

The subject of evil, pain, and suffering has long been used as a weapon of attack against God's existence. With the intent of proselytizing and spreading their hopeless view by attempting to destroy the credibility of God and His Word (something Peter tells us is bound to fail [1 Pet. 1:24-25]), militant atheists assert that a loving God would never allow people to hurt and to go through great pain. However, as we mature in our knowledge of God's pursuits, we understand that it's through Christians choosing to endure suffering while remaining faithful that testifies not only to the existence of God but also the goodness of God. If Christians abandon the faith when sufferings occur, it would be a statement that the Gospel of Jesus Christ is not very valuable. Instead, when a Christian remains faithful, enduring great tribulation, God is glorified, and some may even be won to the Lord.

Why will there be suffering?

In the book of Job, we learn of a righteous man Job who suffered immensely. His pain and anguish supersede anything most of us will ever experience. Family death, financial ruin, and physical ailments were all experienced by this one man who is described in Job 1:1 as *"blameless, upright, fearing God and turning away from evil."* In verse 8, God said of Job, *"There is no one like him on the earth, a blameless and upright man, fearing God and turning away from evil."* Again in Job 2:3, this same description is repeated; however, this statement is added by God in a conversation with Satan, *"And he still holds fast his integrity, although you incited Me against him to ruin him without cause."* The statement *"without cause"* in Job 2:3 needs to be impressed in our minds. The suffering Job experienced was not because of his evil or cause.

> **WHEN A CHRISTIAN REMAINS FAITHFUL, ENDURING GREAT TRIBULATION, GOD IS GLORIFIED.**

In his deep agony, Job is visited by three friends who seek to comfort him; however, because their view of suffering is slanted, their observations and subsequent advice are also slanted. His friend Eliphaz counsels Job regarding his need to repent before God because his sin must be the reason all this calamity is upon him. In Job 4:7-8 we read Eliphaz saying, *"Remember now, who ever perished being innocent? Or where were the upright destroyed? According to what I have seen, those who plow iniquity. And those who sow trouble harvest it."* In other words, he claims this suffering would not happen if Job had repented. Job's friend Bildad counsels Job in chapter 8, verse 20, by saying, *"Lo, God will not reject a man of integrity, nor will He support the evildoers."* His third friend, Zophar, repeats this same slanted admonition in Job 11:14-15 by saying, *"If iniquity is in your hand, put it far away, and do not let wickedness dwell in your tents; Then, indeed, you could lift up your face without moral defect, and you would be steadfast and not fear."* In every single occasion, there is an assumption that suffering only occurs to those who rebel against God. They could not have been more incorrect and less helpful to Job.

The truth is those who suffer don't all suffer for the same reasons. Peter points this out in 1 Peter 2:20 when he writes, *"For what credit is there if, when you sin and are harshly treated, you endure it with patience? But if when you do what is right and suffer for it you patiently endure it, this finds favor with God."* We can clearly discern that there will be times of suffering for doing what's wrong. That's exactly what we see in the perfect example in the lives of the thieves who hung on the crosses on either side of Jesus. One of the thieves even made a statement to this end when trying to silence the rebuke of the other criminal on the cross, he said, *"And we indeed are suffering justly, for we are receiving what we deserve for our deeds; but this man has done nothing wrong"* (Lk. 23:41). However, as Peter stated and the thief on the cross affirmed, there will be times of suffering when you did nothing evil to deserve it. You did what was good and righteous, yet suffering is still cast upon you just like it was upon the shoulders of Jesus.

If you and I fully surrender to God's pursuits in complete submission, we will encounter suffering for the sake of our faith. In our text of 1 Peter 3, two statements are made that truly give us a clearer perspective of the pursuits of God in suffering. In our surrender to His pursuits, we must not shy away from or retreat when we are blessed to be counted worthy to suffer in and for His name. Let's look more closely at these two statements.

- **1 Peter 3:14**—"*But even if you should suffer **for the sake of righteousness**, you are blessed*" (emp. added).

According to *The Complete Word Study Dictionary: New Testament*, in this text, the word *righteousness* means "conformity to the claims of higher authority and stands in opposition to *anomía*, lawlessness."[8] Just as Matthew does in Matthew 5:10-12, Peter emphasizes that some will suffer for doing nothing other than following Jesus Christ. Darkness hates the Light (Jn. 3:19-21), and when we walk in the Light (1 Jn. 1:7), we have a target on our very being. As Christians who live faithfully before God, we will always stand out when we stand up. Our differences will be highlighted when our lives don't fit our communities' standards. That doesn't mean we go looking for trouble; however, it does mean that different people are different, and we are different.

- **1 Peter 3:17**—"*For it is better, **if God should will it so**, that you suffer for doing what is right rather than for doing what is wrong*" (emp. added).

This text might possibly be one of the most difficult for us to swallow as humans because our natural inclination is to reflect on our suffering in light of how uncomfortable it makes us. We struggle with the concept that God could will that we do suffer, and that's just not in our reality when we consider how God loves us. However, when we fall into this snare and begin focusing on ourselves, we realize that we haven't fully surrendered to the pursuits of God in every aspect of our lives. God's pursuits are not for our comforts here in this life. Rather, His pursuits are for the souls of men to be redeemed from the bondage of sin and rescued from the domain of darkness. In that, He may determine that our suffering would be the most effective way to reach a culture as a whole or even an individual who observes how we walk through the fire of difficulty. When you obey the Gospel, you surrender. That includes to the pursuits of God, even in your suffering.

WRAP-UP: SURRENDER TO HIS PURSUITS

Martin James Monti may not be a name that comes to mind when thinking about WWII heroes or even villains. However, this soldier, this traitor to America, is an applicable case study regarding how one transitions from being an enemy combatant to being a fellow soldier. It is truly mind-boggling to think about a person doing what Monti did. In a military sense, it is not usually looked at favorably; however, that's precisely what surrendering to the pursuits of God looks like.

The goal of God is not that we would simply stop living a life of sin but that we would pick up the weapons He outlines in Ephesians 6 and engage as one of His soldiers in this spiritual battle. If that's going to happen, our conversion must also deal with surrendering our minds to God's pursuits. His desires must become our desires. We must change from what we want to a mind and heart that wants what He wants. When this happens, the next step in surrender—arming ourselves to fight the good fight—will be the progression we desire.

FIELD NOTES >>> SURRENDER TO HIS PURSUITS

1. Briefly discuss or consider the opening statement from C.S. Lewis, "The full acting out of the self's surrender to God therefore demands pain; this action, to be perfect, must be done from the pure will to obey, in the absence, or in the teeth, of inclination." What thoughts come to mind when you read this?

2. Before a soldier begins to fight to advance the pursuits of the side he once fought against, what must happen in the soldier's mind? We always hear that I am convinced, or some say convicted, but what does that mean? What must happen inside the soldier who decides to fight against the side he once fought with?

3. In what ways can God use marriages to advance His pursuits? Why would marriage even be something addressed in 1 Peter chapter 3? Of all the different aspects of the lives of these Christians, why would the marriage relationship be addressed?

4. If we are people who tend to want to avoid pain, why is pain and suffering something we are to live expecting as we walk according to the will of God? Briefly think about and describe what has to happen inside the mind of the person who has accepted that suffering for doing what is right is part of his reality.

5. Briefly discuss the phrase in 1 Peter 3:17, "if God should will it so." This concept concerns the Christian suffering in this life for standing for God. Why would God allow suffering to be a part of the reality of mankind while we are on this earth?

"WE DO NOT SEGMENT OUR LIVES, GIVING SOME TIME TO GOD, SOME TO OUR BUSINESS OR SCHOOLING, WHILE KEEPING PARTS TO OURSELVES. THE IDEA IS TO LIVE ALL OF OUR LIVES IN THE PRESENCE OF GOD, UNDER THE AUTHORITY OF GOD, AND FOR THE HONOR AND GLORY OF GOD. THAT IS WHAT THE CHRISTIAN LIFE IS ALL ABOUT."

- R.C. SPROUL[1]

BRIEFING — SURRENDER TO HIS WILL

The laying down of one's weapon as an enemy combatant is significant. Doing so recognizes the hopelessness of fighting against the inevitable loss, yet it also attests to the strength of the conquering authority. However, we have been discussing something more significant in the surrender throughout 1 Peter. When once-enemy combatants are convicted in their core that the purpose and pursuits of God are best, so much so that they arm themselves, not to fight against God but to fight for His will to be advanced even at their own expense and suffering, you know a total surrender demonstrated through submission has been accomplished.

However, as one combs through the pages of military world history, it's difficult to find examples of those who switched allegiances because they believed the other side had it right. Usually, when treason or picking up weapons against one's original side of loyalty has taken place, it is for very self-serving and self-elevating purposes, with money and power being dangled in front of the deserters, scheming and plotting lay behind motives and actions. What may seem like a change of heart was just taking advantage of what appeared to be a better opportunity or an escape from suffering. Consider the following examples.

1. **Alcibiades, Athenian politician and general** (450 – 404 B.C.)
   Early in the Peloponnesian War against Sparta, Alcibiades won a reputation for courage and military talent. By 420 B.C., he had become one of Athen's generals, and in 415 B.C., he persuaded Athens to invade Sicily and conquer Syracuse. However, after it

was suspected that his band of soldiers had desecrated statues of the god Hermes, Alcibiades fled and defected to Sparta to avoid facing a trial before the Athenian Assembly.

In joining the Spartan efforts, he advised and helped organize a strategy that destroyed the army he once led. This short-lived stint with the Spartans came to a crashing halt as Alcibiades was caught in an immoral, compromising situation with the king's wife, so he fled to Persia, where he manipulated their involvement for his gain as well, making sure Athens and Sparta remained too busy fighting one another. After a short and opportunistic rejoining of the Athenians, Alcibiades would ultimately flee for his life to Phrygia, where the Persian governor would murder him in 404 B.C.[2]

2. Flavius Josephus, Jewish general, leader, and historian
(37 – 100 A.D.)

The Great Jewish Revolt erupted in 66 A.D. after the Roman authorities responded to tax protests by arresting prominent Jews and looting the Jewish Temple in Jerusalem. Josephus, a 29-year-old priest in Galilee, was chosen to lead a group of men. After its early setbacks, the empire rebounded under the command of the Roman general Vespasian. With his son Titus, Vespasian marched his legions from Syria into Judea, with Galilee as his first stop.

The men led by Josephus fled to the hilltop town of Jotapata. There, Vespasian surrounded Josephus and his men and successfully stormed the town after a 47-day siege. Having fled to a secret hiding place in a well, Josephus surrendered to the Romans and was taken to Vespasian. Claiming to be a prophet, Josephus said he saw a vision where Vespasian became emperor of Rome, which eventually occurred after Nero's death. With this happening, Josephus was freed from prison. In 70 A.D., along with Titus, he joined the Roman army in the siege of Jerusalem, which ultimately ended in the complete destruction of the temple and the imprisonment of tens of thousands of his fellow countrymen.[3]

3. Japanese warrior, general, and statesman Ashikaga Takauji (1305 – 1358)

In 1333, Takauji was tasked by the Hojos, the ruling clan in Japan, with ending a civil war against Japan's figurehead emperor; however, he preferred the emperor, which resulted in him switching allegiance. With Takauji's help, the Hojos were defeated.

After the emperor was reseated, Takauji was accused of having murdered an imperial prince while he was fighting for the Hojos. Thus, he turned on the emperor and, with military force, again reduced the emperor to a figurehead. At this point, at the age of 33, Takauji founded the Ashikaga Shogunate, which ruled the country from 1338 to 1573.[4]

4. French Revolutionary general Jean-Baptiste Jules Bernadotte (1763 – 1844)

Bernadotte first encountered Napoleon in 1797, after having had great success for the French in battlefronts that included Germany and Italy. The two developed an early friendship after Napoleon declared himself ruler of the empire and Bernadotte swore allegiance to him. As a result, Napoleon appointed Bernadotte a Marshall of France. However, things began to sour between the two during the Prussian campaign in 1806, when Napoleon harshly criticized Bernadotte for failing to lead his men to the battles of

Jena and Auerstadt. In 1809 at the Battle of Wagram, Napoleon relieved Bernadotte of command and sent him back to Paris for "health reasons," a way for Bernadotte to save face.

In 1810, King Charles XIII of Sweden adopted Bernadotte as his heir and thus made him Crown Prince to the throne. Bernadotte eventually assumed the throne of Sweden and sought an accomplishment to solidify his authority and future dynasty. The opportunity came when Napoleon was weakened following his catastrophic invasion of Russia in 1812. In 1813, Bernadotte switched sides, signed a treaty with Britain, and declared war on France. In alliance with the Austrians, Russians, and Prussians, Bernadotte got his payback against Napoleon by helping defeat him in the war's most significant and bloodiest battle, at Leipzig, in 1813.[5]

5. Benedict Arnold, America's most notorious turncoat
(1741 – 1801)

A significant influence in the early days of the American Revolutionary War, Arnold played a leading role in multiple combat efforts, separating himself from the other commanders and showing his excellent leadership skills. With such success, he was marked as a hero; however, his fame aroused fellow officers' resentment and jealousy.

In 1777, in a battle with the British, the now major general Arnold suffered a severe wound that sidelined him from the battlefield. He was given a commission in Philadelphia, where he socialized with loyalist families and lived a very lavish lifestyle. During this time, his financial mismanagement led to scandal and the incurrence of serious debt, as did the spending habits of his young wife who was a loyalist and used to living an extremely extravagant lifestyle. Arnold secretly approached the British in this state, offering to switch sides.

After his stint in charge of Philadelphia, Arnold was put in command of West Point, a fortified position on the Hudson River. He schemed to sell the British plans of the fortifications and to help deliver them into their hands for 20,000 pounds. However, his British contact Major John Andre was captured, along with documents, thus revealing Arnold's intent. Having barely escaped capture at the hands of the Americans, Arnold joined the British and eventually was made a brigadier general in the British army, leading Redcoats against his former army.[67]

Surrendering or changing sides for selfish gain is just self-preservation. There is something within us that seeks to survive and do so in the absence of as much pain and discomfort as possible. Often, we strive diligently to move up in the ranks of society, and we strive for the next promotion, not for the boss's benefit. No, our motivation is because there is something better in it for us—a raise, better hours, or perhaps more time off.

That's why what Peter is teaching the disciples in chapter four is so difficult and thus necessary for admonition to be rendered. As disciples of Jesus, we are called to go against our natural inclinations. Our main priority is no longer our advancement or even the bettering of our family. Those are valid priorities; however, they do not come before our primary motivation of glorifying God in our suffering. When we changed sides when we were converted, we died to ourselves and now we live for Him and the advancement of His will.

INTEL >>> SURRENDER TO HIS WILL

When an individual embraces a new approach to life, everything is different. For instance, when a person goes to the doctor and finds out he has high blood pressure or diabetes and that without a lifestyle change he will die, things change. Sugar-free becomes a reality, and carbohydrates suddenly are a treat. Sleeping late will not help with the problem, so now it's up early and off to the gym or walking around the neighborhood. Now, with a complete change in urgency and purpose regarding lifestyle, this individual is poised to make a difference in his health. However, not everyone responds this way. This is case study number one. The person who is changing everything because he has bought in completely.

The second case study is better but not that different. This person is the one who goes to the doctor and gets the same report. His blood pressure is high, and diabetes has settled in. If something doesn't drastically change, there will be greater health problems soon. This person intellectually knows all of this, but the daily chore of reading food labels, putting different kinds of food in the shopping cart, and developing a new liking for healthier foods are daunting tasks. He's not opposed to exercise; however, the mornings are challenging, so he's very inconsistent at best. In other words, he believes the cost he must pay is too high for the needed healthy results. If you were to describe his approach to a healthy lifestyle change, you would say that he believes something needs to change, but he's not willing to be "all in" and fully commit.

The third case study is the extreme opposite of case study number one. The individual goes to the doctor and gets the same report. He's not feeling well because of the high blood pressure, and diabetes has started to cause neuropathy in his feet. He knows it would be good if his lifestyle changed; however, he likes the food he has become accustomed to and refuses to alter his diet. His approach to exercise is that it is for the young people who care about their looks, so he won't suddenly become superficial like he perceives the exercise crowd to be. Instead, he's not going to change anything and simply live with the expectation that his health will deteriorate just like it's supposed to with age.

Three completely different responses to the need for a lifestyle change. The news in all three is the same, but their level of commitment to change stands out. While the response in case study two is better than in number three, the truth is that neither two nor three exhibit action that communicates a surrender to the lifestyle change. The individual in case study number one shows the only true, complete, "all-in" response. Because of his actions, we can conclude he is the only one who has genuinely changed.

Envision the same three responses as we consider the subject of surrendering to the will of God. If an individual says they have surrendered, but he sits back and continues doing what he's always done, the truth is, he may acknowledge the inevitable outcome of his sinful actions, but he has not surrendered to the will of God. If an individual picks and chooses what aspects of the will of God he likes and thus half-heartedly accommodates, he still has not surrendered. The only response that indicates complete surrender is one that completely acknowledges God is supreme and His will is worth not only one's submission but one's suffering. When one seeks the glory of God above his comforts and even his life, that's when a former enemy combatant has been transformed into a disciple of Jesus Christ.

In our text, Peter explains two critical components to living a life surrendered to the will of God. As we explore them, we should weigh whether these character traits have become who we are or whether they are simply thoughts and ideas we occasionally live with. In other words, are we "all in" in our surrender to the will of God, or do we fall into the same mindset as the individuals in case studies two and three?

 LIVE FOR THE WILL OF GOD, NOT THE LUST OF THE FLESH (1 PET. 4:1-11)

In this life, we make several daily choices that reveal our priorities. Many struggle because it seems these choices are made for us as daily responsibilities take precedence. If we are in school, after a night of study and cramming for the exam, we rush out the door to school. If we are in our working years, the morning commute calls our names, and the "rat race" encompasses us as we strive to do our jobs well, all while climbing the ladder of success. If we are retired, the pace of the day may or may not be slower as our days seem to be just as crowded and full as they were in our earlier years. Time is precious, and while we agree that we get to decide how and where we spend this precious commodity, it seems that the bulk has already been allotted.

Along with our time, we also make daily choices regarding where to spend our money. If we say yes to that expensive boat, by default, we are saying no to something else. When we, with imbalance, elevate our children's extra-curricular activities, which often require a substantial amount of money, we may no longer be able to give to the work of the Lord as we could have otherwise done. With all our money decisions, we communicate the level of surrender to the Lord, and plenty of little eyes are watching and learning from our examples.

While there are numerous categories we could delve into which are a part of our daily decisions, the area that Peter focuses on is the most remarkable and most significant of all. It's not that our choices regarding time, energy, money, or any of the numerous categories that fall into this discussion aren't necessary. It's simply that when we decide to cease living to the flesh and without hesitation and reservation live for the will of God, nothing is hidden and the impact will be felt across every facet of our lives.

Peter begins chapter 4 by directing the readers' attention to a subject he has addressed numerous times and stands as the central example for their endurance. Christ has suffered in the flesh, and as His disciples, we must do the same (Matt. 10:24-25). He even points out in verse 12 how this should not surprise them as they would have known of others who came before them, most notably Jesus Christ, who also suffered for following the will of God. However, for reasons that are all too relevant for us today, humans need to be reminded that when you say yes to Jesus, you are by default saying no to a life of unrestrained fleshly indulgence.

It is of interest that if someone is going to live for the will of God and no longer for the lusts of the flesh, specifically those mentioned in verse 3, there must be a change in mindset before there is ever a shift in behavior. Thus, in verse one, Peter writes, "*Therefore, since Christ has suffered in the flesh, arm yourselves also with the same purpose, because he who has suffered in the flesh has ceased from sin.*" This command to "arm yourselves" is equivalent to setting your mind on the fact that suffering will be part of your life from the moment you obey the Gospel until you die. Just as a soldier prepares himself mentally for going into battle, Peter calls these disciples—and thus you and me—to be mentally ready for persecution that will befall those who choose to live for the will of God. This new life as a follower of Jesus will go against many teachings and practices in a culture that teaches the "eat, drink, and be merry" mantra. Therefore, the person who is going to live with this total surrender in submission to the will of God will need to make sure his mind is settled that God's glory is more important than any acceptance by mankind or comforts this life may afford.

Once this new mindset is embraced, the costs are counted, and one is willing to suffer for the will of God, engagement in the cause of Christ occurs. This is when a disciple of Jesus goes on the offense, only this offensive is not meant to cause pain and destruction. Rather, the motivation of this offensive is to bring honor and glory to God and stir within others a desire to seek forgiveness and, after judgment, live eternally in heaven.

Peter explains this strategy in turning from negative behaviors and converting so much so that positive changes occur within. This turning from negative actions means that the disciple of Jesus must stop doing what is not pleasing to God. The positive component of this offensive is seen in the deeds of goodness they are to be engaged with when it comes the treatment of others. Both may or may not be met with opposition; therefore, the admonition of Peter in 1 Peter 4:7 to *"be of sound judgment and sober spirit"* are right in line with the charge in 1 Peter 1:13 to *"prepare your minds for action, keep sober in spirit, fix your hope completely on the grace to be brought to you at the revelation of Jesus Christ."*

In chapter one, Peter spends a great amount of time describing their redemption when he says they have been "born again" (v. 3); therefore, they are not to be *"conformed to the former lusts which were yours in your ignorance"* (v. 14). "Conformed" comes from the Greek word *suschēmatízō*, a word that combines two words: *sún*, meaning "together with," and *schēmatízō*, meaning "to fashion."[8] So he says, do not live as if you are fashioned together with or in the same pattern as your former life which was lived in sin. Instead, they are to *"be holy yourselves also in all your behavior; because it is written, ' You shall be holy, for I am holy"* (vv. 15-16). With their new birth, comes new expectations.

First, consider what Peter says about ceasing the sinful, unrestrained living of their previous lifestyle.

> *For the time already past is sufficient for you to have carried out the desire of the Gentiles, having pursued a course of sensuality, lusts, drunkenness, carousing, drinking parties and abominable idolatries. In all this, they are surprised that you do not run with them into the same excesses of dissipation, and they malign you.* (1 Peter 4:3-4)

- **"sensuality"**—ἀσέλγεια (asélgeia): from aselgés meaning "lasciviousness, license, debauchery, sexual excess, absence of restraint, insatiable desire for pleasure."[9]
- **"lust"**—ἐπιθυμία (epithumía): from epithuméō meaning "to desire greatly"; generally referring to satisfying the carnal appetites[10]
- **"drunkenness"**—οἰνοφλυγία (oinophlugía): from oinophlugéō meaning "to be drunken," which is from oínos, "wine," and phlúō, "to overflow." An extravagant indulgence in long, drawn-out drinking bouts which may induce permanent damage to the body.[11]
- **"caurousing"**—κῶμος (kómos): A feasting, with riotous conduct (Rom. 13:13); revellings (Gal. 5:21; 1 Pet. 4:3); festivities in honor of several gods, especially Bacchus, the god of wine, hence feastings and drunkenness with impurity and obscenity of the grossest kind. Therefore, it always presupposes a festive company and drunken revellers.[12]
- **"drinking parties"**—πότος (pótos): from pínō meaning "to drink." A drinking match, a drunken bout.[13]
- **"abominable idolatries"**—ἀθέμιτος (athémitos): "abominable"—unlawful; εἰδωλολατρίαις (eidōlolatrías)—"idolatries"—picture or copy. It can be used for images of gods but is not the usual term for cultic images (or human statues). When used for images, the idea is that of a reflection of the deity.[14]

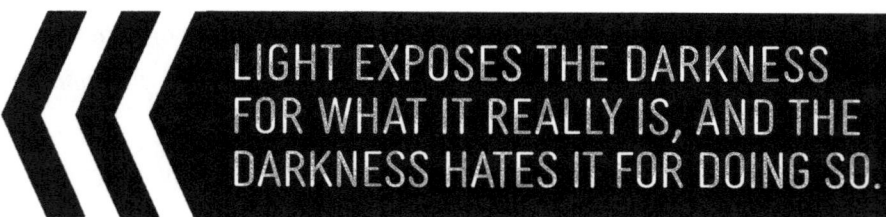

LIGHT EXPOSES THE DARKNESS FOR WHAT IT REALLY IS, AND THE DARKNESS HATES IT FOR DOING SO.

Unfortunately, in a culture where the majority continue to indulge in these same sinful practices, commentary is not needed to expound on these specific sinful practices. However, the one aspect of this verse that is worth looking into deeper is the idea that when people see these Christians are no longer participating in these actions, they are "*surprised.*" This word comes from a Greek word that means "to be surprised, to think something strange."[15] With this, those who observe disciple of Jesus not participating in these evil deeds will respond with malignment. Malign means "*to blaspheme, revile; to hurt the reputation or smite with reports or words, speak evil of, slander, rail.*"[16]

My first reaction to this is, why would they feel like they have to try and hurt the reputation of people who choose not to participate in the same lifestyle? Why couldn't they just leave them alone? After all, who cares if a person who used to be involved in this lifestyle of evil, unrestrained, self-indulgent living decided they no longer wanted to live that way? Why would it matter?

The answer is found in the same reasoning why Jesus was rejected and hated. Darkness loves being in the dark, and when light comes along, hatred springs forth. Light exposes the darkness for what it really is, and the darkness hates it for doing so. Consider the consistent teaching throughout the New Testament on this:

- **Ephesians 5:8**—"*For you were formerly darkness, but now you are Light in the Lord; walk as children of Light.*"
- **John 8:12**—"*Then Jesus again spoke to them, saying, 'I am the Light of the world; he who follows Me will not walk in the darkness, but will have the Light of life.*"

- **John 3:20**—"*For everyone who does evil hates the Light, and does not come to the Light for fear that his deeds will be exposed.*"
- **1 Peter 2:9**—"*But you are a chosen race, a royal priesthood, a holy nation, a people for God's own possession, so that you may proclaim the excellencies of Him who has called you out of darkness into His marvelous light....*"
- **2 Corinthians 6:14**—"*Do not be bound together with unbelievers; for what partnership have righteousness and lawlessness, or what fellowship has light with darkness?*"

While ridding ourselves of these and other negative actions is expected for those who cease to live for the lusts of the flesh, that's not all that is required. God expects a positive internal change as well. In a life where suffering is not a norm, actions consistent with internal change require thought and self-denial. In the face of such great suffering as is being experienced by these disciples, these positive changes not only require putting others above self, they require acting better than you feel. Change demands a focus that is so keen, that even though people may be tempted to think about their pain and discomforts they continually focus on the good of others, especially those who are of the household of God.

Observe the positive internal changes Peter brings to the surface and consider how you're doing in making these your daily default as well.

> *Above all, keep fervent in your love for one another, because love covers a multitude of sins. Be hospitable to one another without complaint. As each one has received a special gift, employ it in serving one another as good stewards of the*

manifold grace of God. Whoever speaks, is to do so as one who is speaking the utterances of God; whoever serves is to do so as one who is serving by the strength which God supplies; so that in all things God may be glorified through Jesus Christ, to whom belongs the glory and dominion forever and ever. Amen. (1 Peter 4: 8-11)

"Love One Another"

This is the word *agape* and denotes a love of decision. It's not based upon another being worthy or deserving of this love. Instead, this love is significant because the one who loves is doing so because it's the best for the one receiving the love. It is also noteworthy that the one loving is to do so fervently, in a continual and intense manner.

"Be Hospitable to One Another"

Hospitality is larger than hosting a meal. While it can include such, truthfully a meal can be shared without hospitality ever being involved. That's because this word means "loving a stranger" or being a "friend to a stranger."[17] Again, there is a clarifier in that they are to have this disposition without complaining or grumbling. It would be much easier if he only wrote to do good deeds to those who are strangers. However, conversion requires genuine change, not merely adherence to good actions.

"Serve One Another"

In our new walk as disciples of Jesus, the grace God has bestowed upon us must be the major driving force in who we've become. With such a gift, a blessing that changes everything, we are to look for ways to shower great blessings on others. Peter explains to these Christians that they have been uniquely blessed by God with talents and abilities which they should seek to use for the benefit of others. This is their default disposition, not a selective, "mission-trip minded" approach. Likewise, we have been blessed with certain skills, and with dedication and diligent pursuit, we have honed these over years of study and usage. Because we have been blessed so richly with the grace of God, our default disposition must be to serve others as stewards of such tremendous grace.

"Speak as One Speaking the Utterances of God'
These disciples are to advance the will of God through their speaking as well. People reveal a lot about themselves by what they say and how they say it. If they are continually talking about themselves, one would logically conclude they are self-centered. If they are constantly advancing by their speech a philosophy they love, one can draw a conclusion that certain philosophers have truly shaped their thinking. However, people also reveal a lot about themselves in what they don't say as well. If people don't speak up against an evil deed or an injustice, one may conclude they are either cowardly or that they agree with the evil. Also, when people spend so much time in their speech advancing the will of God, one will logically conclude that God is not a fringe portion of their lives. Instead, when He saturates their speech like a fountain flowing freely, a person can't help but speak the utterances of God revealed in His Word, it reveals just how much he's gotten into the Word and how much the Word has gotten into him.

As was stated earlier, the motivation for this complete change and conversion is not rooted in what man receives. Rather, it's deeply seated and grounded in one's desire to glorify God through Jesus

Christ (1 Peter 4:11). Our main motive is not what we get out of surrendering, but our wanting our entire life to be about bringing honor and glory to God.

 ENTRUST YOUR SOUL TO GOD IN DOING WHAT IS RIGHT (1 PET. 4:12-19)

Have you ever thought that the difficulties you suffer in life could be the best thing that could have ever happened to you? Believe me, this sounds crazy as I type it, but throughout the Bible, we see some of God's greatest works being done in the lives of His people through the difficulties they were blessed to face. Consider the captivity of the Israelites in Egyptian bondage, the continual roller coaster of the period of the judges, and the horrible period of Babylonian captivity. In each of these, God allowed great suffering; however, all of it was done to turn the hearts of people to God, which is the only source of ultimate good in their lives.

Some may argue that without suffering, we don't fully appreciate peace. It's like without the storm, some may take for granted the calm of the day. If we don't know sickness, we may take for granted good health. If we never do without, we may become spoiled and never fully appreciate living with much. We are fickle as humans, and God knows this. So, instead of doing whatever we can to escape the suffering, Peter tells the disciples to embrace suffering for the right cause and entrust their souls to the One who is faithful and is above all creation (1 Pet. 4:19).

Consider this text and notice the thought process Peter calls followers of Jesus to root deeply in their minds. Without these, it would become very tempting to do whatever is necessary to avoid the persecution. After all, we tend to avoid pain and discomfort at great lengths, but that may not be God's will in your life (1 Pet. 3:17). So, consider how a person can approach persecution so great that in this text it is described as a "fiery ordeal " (1 Pet. 4:12).

> Beloved, **do not be surprised** at the fiery ordeal among you, which comes upon you for your testing, as though some strange thing were happening to you; but to the degree that you share the sufferings of Christ, **keep on rejoicing**, so that also at the revelation of His glory you may rejoice with exultation. If you are reviled for the name of Christ, **you are blessed**, because the Spirit of glory and of God rests on you. Make sure that none of you suffers as a murderer, or thief, or evildoer, or a troublesome meddler; but if anyone suffers as a Christian, **he is not to be ashamed, but is to glorify God** in this name. For it is time for judgment to begin with the household of God; and if it begins with us first, what will be the outcome for those who do not obey the gospel of God? And if it is with difficulty that the righteous is saved, what will become of the godless man and the sinner? Therefore, those also who suffer according to the will of God shall entrust their souls to a faithful Creator in doing what is right. (1 Peter 4: 12-19, emp. added)

- **I Will Not Live with the Surprise of Suffering—"Do not be surprised"** Surprises have a way of derailing people, and the only way to deal with a surprise or the shock of an event are to mentally prepare oneself as much as possible to expect the negative to happen. In verse 12, Peter is not saying that Christians should live with a "gloom-and-doom" approach that clouds every day of their lives. To the contrary, since, as disciples of Jesus Christ and heirs to the promises of God, we have a living hope (1 Pet. 1:3) guaranteed by the living God in His living Word (1 Pet. 1:23).

When as Christians we live with the expectation of suffering for the name of Christ, mentally it's doesn't come as a surprise. While it doesn't take away the sting of the trial, living with this expectation allows us to prepare to handle and respond to such in a manner that seeks to bring honor and glory to God. In that, we are blessed when we remember those who have gone before us who have endured so much for the name of Jesus.

- **I Will Find Joy in the Privilege of Suffering for Jesus—"Keep on rejoicing"** Finding joy amidst hardship takes a tremendously settled outlook on one's destination and purpose. When we find our joys in this life only and they are taken away, our countenance dissipates and can be destroyed. However, when a person has stored his treasure in Heaven, where moth and rust cannot destroy nor thieves break in and steal (Matt. 6:19-22), one's heart and the joy therein are settled beyond reach of the persecution of men. Disciples can be threatened, beaten, or even killed; however, their investment is in the eternal and their focus remains settled there. Therefore, as they encounter great trials in this life because they choose to follow Jesus and live for the will of God, they take joy in that they are intimately linked to Jesus through suffering.

- **I Will Maintain an Eternal Focus Through Suffering—"You are blessed"** In this text, the word *blessed* means "possessing the favor of God."[18] I'll be the first to admit it is extremely difficult to see any blessing in suffering; however, just as we considered when looking at *"keep on rejoicing,"* as Christians, our treasure is not stored here on this earth. Like those in the book of Hebrews, we *"seek a better country"* (Heb. 11:16). It's that focus beyond this world and whatever we may encounter here that causes the disciple of Jesus to hold fast when the storms of persecution rage.

The one who does this without caving and wavering is the one who possesses the favor of God, and this favor is not to be considered haphazardly. Instead, this favor is a major component of one's willing endurance under the tremendous weight of suffering. That's what Jesus said in the Sermon on the Mount when we read, *"Blessed are those who have been persecuted for the sake of righteousness, for theirs is the kingdom of heaven. Blessed are you when people insult you and persecute you, and falsely say all kinds of evil against you because of Me. Rejoice and be glad, for your reward in heaven is great; for in the same way they persecuted the prophets who were before you"* (Matt. 5:10-12).

> **FINDING JOY AMIDST HARDSHIP TAKES A TREMENDOUSLY SETTLED OUTLOOK ON ONE'S DESTINATION AND PURPOSE.**

- **I Will Not Be Ashamed Because I Am Suffering—"He is not to be ashamed"** Dishonoring someone is a serious slap in the face. When Jesus was struck during His unjust trials, not only were the soldiers attempting to hurt Him, but they were also mocking Him publicly as they sought His shame. However, shame is something that some may try and assign to another, but it doesn't have to be embraced by the one they are attempting to burden. Even as the crowd mocked Him and reviled Him, our Savior continued embracing and entrusting Himself to the Father instead of embracing the shame that was being cast at Him. That's a demonstration of great power, focus, and confidence in the One who ultimately is in control when shame of this world isn't embraced by the one suffering. When the persecutors cannot do anything to cause you to be embrace shame or be ashamed, the power they think they have over you only shows how great their weakness truly is.

There are many verses in the New Testament regarding the subject of being ashamed. For our benefit in seeing a bigger picture on this subject, let's consider a few of them.

- **Mark 8:38**—"*For whoever is **ashamed** of Me and My words in this adulterous and sinful generation, the Son of Man will also be ashamed of him when He comes in the glory of His Father with the holy angels*" (emp. added).

- **Romans 1:16**—"*For I am not **ashamed** of the gospel, for it is the power of God for salvation to everyone who believes, to the Jew first and also to the Greek*" (emp. added).

- **2 Timothy 1:12**—"*For this reason I also suffer these things, but I am not **ashamed**; for I know whom I have believed and I am convinced that He is able to guard what I have entrusted to Him until that day*" (emp. added).

- **Hebrews 11:16**—"*But as it is, they desire a better country, that is, a heavenly one. Therefore God is not **ashamed** to be called their God; for He has prepared a city for them*" (emp. added).

- **I Will Seek to Bring Glory to God Through Suffering—"Glorify God"** "To glorify God, meaning to render glory to Him, recognize Him for Who and What He is, to celebrate with praises, worship, adoration."[19] That's what is written in the *Complete Word Study Dictionary* regarding the usage of this word *glory*. Incredible! When one is suffering, his mindset is to continually going back to how good and powerful God is. That's why Peter brings to the mind of the readers just who God is and why He's worthy of us seeking His glory.

He is the Owner of the household (1 Pet. 4:17) and the Opposer of the proud (5:5). He is the Creator (4:19) and the great Re-Creator, demonstrated in our being "*born again*" through the blood of Jesus (1:3). He is the Protector of our inheritance (1:5) and the Resurrector of our Savior (1:21). He is the God of Patience (3:20) and Purveyor of the Gospel (4:17).

Repeatedly, the apostle Peter explains why God is worthy of their suffering and why His will is to be sought far above their own. The disciples receiving this letter needed to remember that. To have clarity of mind when there is peace or at least very little cost to following Jesus, is one thing. However, when the fires of purification and persecution intensify, what truly believes about who God is rises to the surface. For these Christians, and I hope for us today, the nature of God and the living hope of spending eternity with Him is why they "*entrust their souls*" or "place with someone for one's own sake, to give in charge, to commit, entrust" to God.[20] We would say they surrender in submission to His will and in so doing, God, the One so well described in 1 Peter as the Securer of that great reservation in eternity (1 Pet. 1:4), will be faithful to His promises.

★ WRAP-UP ≫ SURRENDER TO HIS WILL

When we contemplate the concept of surrender through submission as the Scriptures teach, we must also come to a more mature understanding of the reasons behind our transformation. God's promise to us of eternal salvation is without question a key component to why anyone would lay down his weapons once used to fight against God as he lived a life of unrestricted self-fulfilling pleasure. However, a change of sides for the sole sake of selfish gain is self-seeking, and the Scriptures teach that following God is not about the elevation of self or selfish gain (Phil. 2:4; Jas. 3:16; Lk. 9:23). Instead, we are to surrender, not only in ceasing to do evil, but we are also, with correct, God-honoring motives, to engage in doing good stemming from an internal change. In 1 Peter, the motivation we accept and embrace in surrender through submission is so that **God will be glorified.** Our main motive is not what we get out of surrendering, but it matures to our wanting our entire lives to be about bringing honor and glory to God.

> *Whoever speaks, is to do so as one who is speaking the utterances of God; whoever serves is to do so as one who is serving by the strength which God supplies; so that in all things God may be glorified through Jesus Christ, to whom belongs the glory and dominion forever and ever. Amen. (*1 Peter 4:11)

FIELD NOTES >> SURRENDER TO HIS WILL

1. Think about self-preservation. We will do what it takes to see that this happens in our lives. However, how does this concept play into people obeying the Gospel? Is it appropriate for self-preservation to be the main reason or a major driving force behind someone surrendering to the will of God?

2. Why is it so difficult to embrace a different approach to life? For instance, this chapter's illustration was about three men who received a bad report from the doctor. In each, there is a different response. Why do you think it's difficult to accept that life will be different from that moment on? What all must be processed if change and embracing another way is going to occur?

3. In your life, how have you done with not living for the flesh? That question just cuts right to it; however, let's get to it instead of discussing everything we shouldn't do in the flesh. How are you doing in this area of your life, and why is that the case? What is holding you back from truly surrendering to the will of God?

4. Why do you think so many Christians are surprised that the world doesn't agree with them? How does preparing one's mind for difficult times help them when they encounter them?

5. As self-preservation has been discussed throughout this chapter, it's fitting that it ends with counting it a privilege to suffer for the sake of Jesus. How hard is this in your life, and what seems to be your struggle in counting it a privilege to suffer for Jesus? Since it is a privilege, do you avoid the suffering, or have you embraced shining brightly for His cause?

"LET GOD HAVE YOUR LIFE;
HE CAN DO MORE WITH IT
THAN YOU CAN."

- DWIGHT L. MOODY[1]

BRIEFING

SURRENDER TO HIS MIGHTY HAND

The Charge of the Light Brigade[2]
By Alfred Lord Tennyson
December 9, 1854

Half a league, half a league,
Half a league onward,
All in the valley of Death
Rode the six hundred.
"Forward, the Light Brigade!
Charge for the guns!" he said.
Into the valley of Death
 Rode the six hundred.

"Forward, the Light Brigade!"
Was there a man dismayed?
Not though the soldier knew
Someone had blundered.
Theirs not to make reply,
Theirs not to reason why,
Theirs but to do and die.
Into the valley of Death
Rode the six hundred.

Cannon to right of them,
Cannon to left of them,
Cannon in front of them
Volleyed and thundered;
Stormed at with shot and shell,
Boldly they rode and well,
Into the jaws of Death,
Into the mouth of hell
Rode the six hundred.

Flashed all their sabres bare,
Flashed as they turned in air
Sabring the gunners there,
Charging an army, while
All the world wondered.
Plunged in the battery-smoke
Right through the line they broke;
Cossack and Russian
Reeled from the sabre stroke
Shattered and sundered.
Then they rode back, but not
Not the six hundred.

Cannon to right of them,
Cannon to left of them,
Cannon behind them
Volleyed and thundered;
Stormed at with shot and shell,
While horse and hero fell.
They that had fought so well
Came through the jaws of Death,
Back from the mouth of hell,
All that was left of them,
Left of six hundred.

When can their glory fade?
O the wild charge they made!
All the world wondered.
Honour the charge they made!
Honour the Light Brigade,
Noble six hundred!

On October 25, 1854, during the Crimean War between Russia and the allied forces comprised of Britain, France, and Turkey (1853-1856), what has become infamously known as "The Charge of the Light Brigade" historically unfolded as a few more than 600 British calvary charged toward a Russian heavy artillery stronghold through what is known as the North Valley near the port city of Balaklava. Under the command of Lord Raglan, commander of British forces, Lord Cardigan, commander of the Light Brigade, received a simple and firm order to charge the enemy artillery line. This was to prevent further retreat and repositioning of the cannons, a maneuver being undertaken by the Russian forces due to the victories of the more heavily armored British calvary unit known as the Heavy Brigade just a few hours prior to this engagement. While this was the command Cardigan received, the initial command from Raglan was very different. Tasked with the delivery of the written order, Captain Louis Nolan verbally interpreted the command to charge as immediate and to be directed at the most substantial portion of the Russian forces about a mile through a gauntlet known as the North Valley; however, that is not what Lord Raglan intended.

Thinking the order to be careless and absurd as it would have made more sense to attack the isolated Russian forces that surrounded the valley instead of charging his soldiers into inevitable death and destruction, Cardigan, with a soldier's resolve to follow orders of a superior officer, had to obey what he thought were Raglan's wishes. Moving from a slow advance to a full charge, the Light Brigade consumed the fire from the Russians on the heights of the valley. Being surrounded on three sides, the British soldiers bravely charged ahead, taking on heavy losses as bullets and cannonballs rained upon them. By the time they reached the Russian battery, after having lost men and horses due to injury or death, they now faced the real threat of being entirely encapsulated by the Russians due to Lord Raglan's decision to hold back the Heavy Brigade to reinforce the initial charge because of the heavy losses already suffered in this horrific maneuver.

The Russians noticed no reinforcements were charging, so they swiftly moved from their high position into the valley. Noticing the lack of a second wave, the Light Brigade battled gallantly through the Russian line behind them in a desperate retreat. However, the damage to one of the greatest weapons of the allied forces in the Crimean War—the Light Brigade—was already suffered. Of the little over 600 men who charged into the valley, 110 were killed, about 130 were wounded, and another 30 were injured or captured. Along with the significant loss of men, around 375 horses were also killed or had to be put down due to their wounds.

The deathly charge and ensuing melee lasted merely 20 minutes and was over by noon; however, the legacy of the Light Brigade lives on to this day. Although the British suffered a significant setback and defeat at this turn in the Crimean War, they hailed the heroic survivors of the charge as a symbol of their army's courage and perseverance. Poet and, in a manner, historian Alfred, Lord Tennyson cemented the legacy of the Light Brigade beyond the British empire when less than two full months after the brutal charge he wrote what has become one of the most infamous lines in all of poetry: "*Theirs not to make reply, Theirs not to reason why, Theirs but to do and die.*"[3]

What is it within a soldier that would cause him, knowing the terrible odds of his own life being ripped away from him, to charge through a gauntlet of heavy artillery and look his mortality dead in the eyes? The charge of the Light Brigade is not an isolated case. Rare, yes, but not the only time in warfare that we see soldiers gallantly follow their superior's command, knowing doing so will most likely cost their lives. But what is it within a person that allows for such a submissive response?

Up to this point, we have considered our initial condition as enemy combatants of God (Rom. 5:10) due to our decision to live in sinful darkness and the progression of transformation that takes place in our lives as we lay our weapons down in obedience to the Gospel and "buy in" to the purpose and pursuits of God. We have considered what true surrender through submission entails and how Peter admonishes the scattered recipients of this letter not merely to lay their weapons down but to engage in the cause of Christ, advancing the will of God. Now, as we turn our attention to the fifth chapter of 1 Peter, just like the courageous soldiers of the Light Brigade at Balaklava we come face-to-face with the reality that truly surrendering to God, voluntarily placing ourselves under the mighty hand of God (1 Pet. 5:6), means we may and most likely will suffer for His cause, potentially losing our own lives as we obey.

So, what does it take to charge ahead, knowing the pain and persecution that lies ahead? In this chapter, we learn of two critical character traits that require great resolve and the emptying of selfishness and self-fulfillment in our lives. These vital traits are not ours merely because they are espoused verbally. Our lives and the price we pay indicate whether we have transformed from enemy combatants to the charging soldiers God desires. Counting the cost before the command to charge is ever sounded allowed the Light Brigade soldiers to rush head-first into the heart of the Russian heavy artillery. We must do the same in our obedience to God. Before the bugle ever sounds, we must have a settled resolve that whatever God's mighty hand brings and allows is precisely what is needed for His cause, and just as Lord Tennyson wrote in 1854, as Christians, we do so understanding, *"Theirs not to make reply, Theirs not to reason why, Theirs but to do and die."*

SURRENDER TO HIS MIGHTY HAND

The phrase *"under the mighty hand of God"* (1 Pet. 5:6) intrigues many Bible students. While we understand that God is spirit (Jn. 4:24) and thus does not have literal hands as we do, the disciple's mind can't help but wonder at the meaning of this phrase. After all, if we are to humble ourselves under His mighty hand, we must know and understand what this is and what this phrase truly means in our lives.

Using anthropomorphic language—assigning human qualities to something or someone who is not human—the Holy Spirit, through the pen of various writers of the Bible, ascribes different qualities that humans possess to God, helping us better to understand the nature of God and His immutable attributes. For instance:

- **Hebrews 4:13**—*"And there is no creature hidden from His sight, but all things are open and laid bare to the **eyes of Him** with whom we have to do"* (emp. added)
- **Leviticus 20:6**—*"As for the person who turns to mediums and to spiritists, to play the harlot after them, I will also set **My face** against that person and will cut him off from among his people"* (emp. added)

- **Isaiah 23:11**—"*He has stretched **His hand** out over the sea, He has made the kingdoms tremble; The Lord has given a command concerning Canaan to demolish its strongholds*" (emp. added)
- **2 Kings 19:16**—"*Incline **Your ear,** O Lord, and hear; open Your eyes, O Lord, and see; and listen to the words of Sennacherib, which he has sent to reproach the living God*" (emp. added)
- **Nahum 1:3**—"*The Lord is slow to anger and great in power, And the Lord will by no means leave the guilty unpunished. In whirlwind and storm is His way, And clouds are the dust beneath **His feet**"* (emp. added)

GOD ALLOWS THE FIRES TO PROOF OUR FAITH

So, when we read 1 Peter 5:6 and see the Spirit referring to the mighty hand of God, we must pause and realize this writing technique has been utilized from the Old Testament through the New Testament and isn't meant to be taken literally. There's a more profound message being revealed in this writing method, and we must grasp it if we are to surrender according to the Scripture properly. God is not like us, and remembering this would do us well. The prophet Isaiah emphasizes this when he writes, "*For as the heavens are higher than the earth, So are My ways higher than your ways and My thoughts than your thoughts*" (Is. 55:9). Therefore, to what is the apostle Peter referring when he writes about the mighty hand of God?

As we turn our attention to a general study of the hand/s of God, we find there are over 50 references in both the Old and New Testaments. While each is better understood in its context, we can glean much regarding the meaning of the hands of God by looking at a few.

- **Exodus 14:8**—the help of the Lord
- **Deuteronomy 2:15**—God's resistless power
- **Acts 13:11**—the judgment of God
- **Ezra 7:6**—the providential care of the Lord
- **Psalm 18:35**—the protection afforded by God
- **Psalm 20:6-7**—the saving strength of God
- **Isaiah 41:10**—the promise to uphold

Repeatedly, this reference to the hand of God is used to demonstrate who our God is and how He interacts with His creation. He provides, sustains, and protects. Sustenance is found in His hand, and He will render and administer justice. All of this helps paint a complete picture in our minds of one key component, one key aspect of God's nature that is crucial to our journey to complete surrender. That one pivotal piece of God's character and nature is His omnipotence. It's a word that means "God's unlimited authority to bring into existence or cause to happen whatsoever he wills."[4]

It's this aspect of God that causes the pause mentioned at the beginning of this section because if God is all-powerful, then that means He allows the fires to proof our faith (1 Pet. 1:7). He chooses not to stop the pains of persecution (1 Pet. 1:6) or prevent the beatings of the bullying mobs against His disciples (1 Pet. 3:14). He allows the slashings of slander to cut to the heart of those who love Him (1 Pet. 3:16). He admonishes His disciples to ready themselves to the onslaught against their fleeting flesh at the hands of those who stand in the ranks we once occupied when we were the enemy combatants (1 Pet. 4:1).

In this seeming dilemma, we are forced to willfully swallow this last cold, hard fact of surrender through submission. That pill is that we are not merely to surrender to the will of God but that we are to continually submit through the will of God, even if that means our bodies are beaten, burned, or broken. We are to voluntarily, without question, go where He says go, charge where He says charge, speak what He says speak, and be who He says we are to be. These responses are not laborious when we reach this point in our surrender. While the outcomes on this earth may be unfavorable to us, we now stand in the ranks of the disciples of Jesus Christ and wholly seek His will to be done. To do this, we must allow Him to change us, and that can only occur when we humble ourselves and resist the one who wants to drag us back to the other side.

 IN ORDER TO FULLY SURRENDER, YOU MUST HUMBLE YOURSELF

In 1 Peter 5:5, Peter admonishes the reader to *"clothe yourselves with humility toward one another..."* In verse 6, he echoes this charge, only this time it's in relation to God, "Therefore, humble yourselves under the mighty hand of God." Sandwiched between these two passages dealing with humility, Peter quotes Proverbs 3:34, *"For God is opposed to the proud, but gives grace to the humble."* In doing so, Peter lays down the stark comparison between two great foes, pride, and humility. One that truly is the difference between a temporary elevation in this life and an eternal exaltation that God Himself can only achieve.

This apparent contrast stands as the pinnacle of surrendering to the mighty hand of God and, thus, ultimately, to God in general. Where pride has taken root, humility will always struggle. However,

WHERE PRIDE HAS TAKEN ROOT, HUMILITY WILL ALWAYS STRUGGLE.

when one indeed places himself under the power of God, not merely accepting whatever comes his way but choosing to continue the difficult journey of voluntarily surrendering through the persecutions, fiery ordeal, slander, abuse, or any amount of maltreatment for the sake of advancing the cause of Christ, only then does he have true humility and thus surrender is exemplified. In other words, *"If God should will it so, that you suffer..."* (1 Pet. 3:17), then the one who has humbled himself under the mighty hand of God will *"keep on rejoicing"* (1 Pet. 4:13) through his suffering.

Specifically speaking, in 1 Peter 5, there are three groups of people Peter addresses with these sentiments. The first is the *"elders among you"* (1 Pet. 5:1). Interestingly, Peter places himself alongside this group as a fellow elder. Although, he could have appealed to them as an apostle, thus claiming and forcing apostolic authority. Along with this description, he also points to the fact that he witnessed the sufferings of Christ and was a partaker of the glory to be revealed.

All these descriptions—elder, witness, and partaker—point to the necessity for humility because they hinge on the work of God through Christ. Without Christ suffering and dying on the cruel cross, there is no church and thus no elders. As Peter draws upon being a witness ("one who has information or knowledge of something, and hence, one who can give information, bring to light, or confirm something")[5] of the sufferings of Christ, we can't help but recall that during this time, Peter exhibited a severe lack of humility under the mighty hand of God as he denied knowing Jesus, even cursing in so doing. However, when Peter identifies as a "partaker of the glory that is to be revealed " (v. 1), he boldly declares the rest of the story. Peter's repentance and the charge Jesus gives him can be read about in John 21:15-17.

> *So when they had finished breakfast, Jesus said to Simon Peter, "Simon, son of John, do you love Me more than these?" He said to Him, " Yes, Lord; You know that I love You." He said to him, "Tend My lambs." He said to him again a second time, "Simon, son of John, do you love Me?" He said to Him, " Yes, Lord; You know that I love You." He said to him, "Shepherd My sheep." He said to him the third time, "Simon, son of John, do you love Me?" Peter was grieved because He said to him the third time, "Do you love Me?" And he said to Him, "Lord, You know all things; You know that I love You." Jesus said to him, "Tend My sheep."*

It's fascinating to discover in this text that the shepherding of the sheep Jesus calls Peter to be about is rooted in a love for Jesus. This love is unconditional, meaning our love for Jesus is not based on whether He does what we want Him to do or gives the outcome we desire, and all-encompassing, meaning there is no corner of my life not impacted by my love for Him. Jesus ties Peter's commitment to Him directly to caring for His people, and that's the thrust of what Peter does in 1 Peter 5. The clear picture of the heart, the love, and devotion they have for God and others, is seen in the admonition to shepherd 1) "not under compulsion but voluntarily," 2) *"not for sordid gain but with eagerness,"* and 3) not as *"lording it over"* the sheep but as examples to the flock. After all, these elders are to remember that Jesus is the Chief Shepherd (1 Pet. 5:4), and the flock ultimately belongs to God.

The second group Peter addresses in chapter 5 is the *"younger men"* (v. 5). Scripture characterizes one's youth as a time of energy and strength. The pressures and expectations of youth are often addressed, as are warnings regarding temptations that may seek to ensnare young people. Biblical writers also seek to instruct the young about what is expected of them in this season of their lives. Consider the following passages.

- **Psalm 119:9**—*"How can a young man keep his way pure? By keeping it according to Your word."*
- **Proverbs 20:29**—*"The glory of young men is their strength, And the honor of old men is their gray hair."*
- **Ecclesiastes 11:9–12:1**—*"Rejoice, young man, during your childhood, and let your heart be pleasant during the days of young manhood. And follow the impulses of your heart and the desires of your eyes. Yet know that God will bring you to judgment for all these things. So, remove grief and anger from your heart and put away pain from your body, because childhood and the prime of life are fleeting. Remember also your Creator in the days of your youth, before the evil days come and the years draw near when you will say, 'I have no delight in them."*
- **1 Timothy 4:12**—*"Let no one look down on your youthfulness, but rather in speech, conduct, love, faith and purity, show yourself an example of those who believe."*
- **2 Timothy 2:22**—*"Now flee from youthful lusts and pursue righteousness, faith, love and peace, with those who call on the Lord from a pure heart."*

Within the arena of humility being addressed in 1 Peter 5, there is good reason the Holy Spirit through Peter addresses the category of young men. Sometimes, our youth can cause us to think we know more than we really know. Often in our youth, we see every situation as something to be controlled and manhandled with our energy and strength. We have such a great desire to achieve and accomplish extraordinary outcomes that we may struggle to appreciate the knowledge that comes with the experience the elderly possess. The youth must remember the elderly have lived longer and have more scars. Their vantage point is much different, and therefore, possibly more complete. The advice and direction of those called to shepherd must be heeded, and the Spirit knows there is great potential for conflict between the young toward the elderly. Thus, Peter admonishes the youth to place themselves under the elders willfully. He doesn't call them to argue or even seek clarification from the elders. He simply calls upon them to love the Lord enough to do what pleases Him.

The third group of people Peter addresses in the opening verses of chapter 5 are "all of you" (v. 5). This category is all-encompassing and includes the elders, young men, and all the recipients of this letter. We aren't going to spend much time diving into an explanation or observations surrounding this group, and you can see who they are in 1 Peter 1:1; however, the instruction to "clothe yourselves with humility" (v. 5) is deserving of our attention.

The word used here for "clothe yourselves" is ἐγκομβόομαι (*egkombóomai*) and "means to gather or tie in a knot, hence to fasten a garment, to clothe."[6] An *egkombóomai* is a long white apron or outer garment with strings worn by slaves. It conjures in the mind of the serious Bible student the imagery of Jesus tying the towel of service around His waist as He humbly washed the disciples' feet in John 13.[7] When Peter used this word, he said that humility, the voluntary lowering of oneself, needs not just to be something one occasionally does. Instead, a humble mindset is an outer garment that encompasses everything else. It is to be what is first seen. It is to be the outermost layer of attitude and disposition displayed in how they respond to one another. That's why Peter brings us back to a key verse from the Old Testament—Proverbs 3:34, "*God is opposed to the proud, but gives grace to the humble.*"

 IN ORDER TO FULLY SURRENDER, YOU MUST HUMBLE YOURSELF

When major decisions are made, there always seems to be the possibility of second-guessing that could linger. It could be something as simple as ordering a meal from a menu, and when it arrives at your table, you begin looking at what everyone got and wondering if you should have gotten what they have. It could be as simple as when you're driving and turn right because you have to make a split-second decision. As you continue along the new path, you might second-guess your choice. It could also be more serious such as making a significant purchase. When it was in the showroom, the vehicle looked nice and you had to have it, but when you get it home and drive it for a few days, buyer's remorse may set in and you begin to question whether or not you made the right decision.

In a much more severe context, when following Jesus costs you everything, including your physical comfort, there may be a strong tendency to question if staying on God's side is worth it. After all, at one time, as enemy combatants, we lived comfortably according to the lusts of the flesh (1 Pet. 1:14). Darkness loves darkness and doesn't care if we bask in sin. However, when we surrender to God through submission, everything changes. Satan no longer has a hold on our lives, and it seems he doubles his efforts through temptations and persecutions. That's why Peter writes three imperatives in 1 Peter 5:8-9 he intends for the disciples to accomplish to stay the course, remaining faithful through the storms they are encountering. He tells them to *"be of sober spirit,"* *"be on the alert,"* and *"resist him"* (the devil).

The human mind is fascinating. It can process data at such high speeds, yet it can sometimes misinterpret it because emotions and past experiences can influence it. It's more than merely a computer that takes in data and spits out results. Instead, it's a complicated organ that is continually observing and responding. Chemical processes occur regularly, and neurons fire according to stimuli. When we touch, taste, hear, smell, or see something, signals sent throughout the brain allow us to comprehend the world around us. There are also memory compartments (sensory, short-term, long-term) through which our experiences and observations filter. Once the stimuli are filtered, the brain kicks in our response mechanisms, releasing chemicals, some allowing for positive rewards and others that are negative. We like the peace and calm of the positive; however, we want to avoid the adverse effects.

God knows how He made us and how wonderfully powerful the brain truly is, and He knows that where the mind leads actions are bound to follow. That's why we see the urgency to set our minds on God and His will throughout Scripture. Note the emphasis in these verses.

- **Matthew 22:37**—"And He said to him, ' You shall love the Lord your God with all your heart, and with all your soul, and with all your mind."
- **Mark 8:33**—"But turning around and seeing His disciples, He rebuked Peter and said, 'Get behind Me, Satan; for you are not setting your mind on God's interests, but man's."
- **Romans 8:5-8**—"For those who are according to the flesh set their minds on the things of the flesh, but those who are according to the Spirit, the things of the Spirit. For the mind set on the flesh is death, but the mind set on the Spirit is life and peace, because the mind set on the flesh is hostile toward God; for it does not subject itself to the law of God, for it is not even able to do so, and those who are in the flesh cannot please God."
- **Colossians 3:2**—"Set your mind on the things above, not on the things that are on earth."
- **1 Peter 1:13**—"Therefore, prepare your minds for action, keep sober in spirit, fix your hope completely on the grace to be brought to you at the revelation of Jesus Christ."

Being sober means being "watchful, circumspect."[8] It brings a certain clarity void of intoxicants, either of a physical substance or of negative interpretations of the sufferings that could be used to cloud the Christian's perception. We understand through our observance of Satan's interaction with God in the case of Job that Satan is limited in his abilities. After all, he is not a deity and does not possess the same traits as God. However, in 1 Peter 5:8, he is identified as the "adversary," *antídikos*—from *antí*, "*against*" and *díkē*—a cause or suit at law."[9] In this same text, Satan is referred to as the "*devil*," meaning "he is an accuser and a slanderer."[10] In other words, he is the accuser ready to make a legal claim against Christians before

God. He is also metaphorically referred to as a roaring lion seeking, looking purposefully, for anyone he may consume. This consumption may, and often does, begin in the mind of one who becomes his prey. Where the mind goes, the actions follow.

Thus, Peter echoes the urgency of the settled disposition of the Christians when he tells them to "be alert." The word used here is *grēgoreúō* from *egeírō*, meaning "to arise, arouse; to watch, to refrain from sleep."[11] It denotes "a mindfulness of threatening dangers which, with conscious earnestness and an alert mind, keeps it from all drowsiness and all slackening in the energy of faith and conduct."[12] In other words, as Jesus in the Garden of Gethsemane told Peter, James, and John to keep watch while He went and prayed (Matt. 26:36), Peter is telling us to keep watch with the alertness of mind and attention. Ironically, in the Garden of Gethsemane, Peter and the others fell asleep and were rebuked by Jesus for doing so. In the second charge, Jesus told them, "*Keep watching and praying that you may not enter into temptation; the spirit is willing, but the flesh is weak*" (Matt. 26:41). This is such a true statement, and now as Peter is an older disciple and is instructing Christians how they are to approach the temptations brought about by the intense sufferings, he no doubt draws from his struggle as he speaks to the urgent necessity to "*be alert*."

WHERE THE MIND GOES, THE ACTIONS FOLLOW.

Lastly, as an all-encompassing command, Peter instructs the disciples to "resist him," referring to the devil. The word is *anthístēmi*, from *antí*—"against", and *hístēmi*—to stand.[13] At some point in the life of a person who wants to follow Jesus, there must be a line drawn in the sand where the Christian's resolve and commitment to God are dug in, and the enemy will not push us back anymore. God does care for us (1 Pet. 5:7); therefore, He is more than capable of bearing the weight of our fear and concern. However, He requires more from us than simply saying a prayer and telling ourselves it will all be okay because God sent Jesus to die on the cross. He needs you and me to stand against the devil's schemes actively and with great zeal. Just as a soldier holds the line, God requires that each of us in our individual lives have a determined resolve that even in the face of sufferings from persecution, the devil will not have a playground in our lives. We must be resolved in our discipleship. We serve the King of kings and the Lord of lords (1 Tim. 6:15). Jesus has already rendered the devil powerless in His conquest over the grave (Heb. 2:15). God through Christ has already won the battle; therefore, the words of James are as valid today as they were when he first wrote them, "*Resist the devil, and he will flee from you*" (Jas. 4:7). If it weren't possible, God would not have demanded it from His followers. So the only dilemma before you and me is will we surrender to mighty hand of God in taking a stand in resisting the devil—his attempts to turn us back to darkness, his persecutions that cause us physical pain and suffering, and his lies that try to convince us that it's better if we return to our vomit (Prov. 26:11). Even in the face of a fiery ordeal, our reply to the devil must be one of resolve as was the response of Shadrach, Meshach, and Abednego to Nebuchadnezzar when faced with compromising or suffering in the fiery furnace, "*If it be so, our God whom we serve is able to deliver us from the furnace of blazing fire; and He will deliver us out of your hand, O king. But even if He does not, let it be known to you, O king, that we are not going to serve your gods or worship the golden image that you have set up*" (Dan. 3:17-18).

WRAP-UP — SURRENDER TO HIS MIGHTY HAND

For soldiers to obediently charge into a situation where the odds are incredibly high that pain, suffering, and death are a likely outcome—just as the Light Brigade did during the Battle at Balaklava—those soldiers have to have settled in their minds that the cause for which they lay their lives down is unquestionably worth the sacrifice. If there is doubt or the sense of self- preservation overwhelms them, there is a strong likelihood they will either retreat or not give their best effort. If they begin thinking it would be easier to be on the other side, the side of the enemy combatants, there is a strong likelihood they will be quick to desert. There can be no question that the side they are fighting is right. Their mission is the proper mission. The one for whom they fight is the right one. When this is settled in the soldiers' minds, they will be willing to sacrifice if that is what is required of them, even their lives.

In this journey of surrender through submission, we have marched through the process from starting as an enemy combatant against God Almighty, to buying into the purpose and pursuits of God, then surrendering to His will and now His mighty hand. We now fight on the side of advancing the cause of Christ. Only it's not a war fought with carnal weapons (2 Cor. 10:4). The armor we wear is defensively and offensively designed to deal with the schemes of the devil (Eph. 6:11). As the apostle Paul told the church in Ephesus, *"For our struggle is not against flesh and blood, but against the rulers, against the powers, against the world forces of this darkness, against the spiritual forces of wickedness in the heavenly places"* (Eph. 6:12).

In this spiritual war, tactics are being utilized by the enemy of God that seeks to exploit our temporary, physical nature. The desire of the enemy is that we would be dead (Eph. 2:1), separated from God in the spiritual aspect of our nature.

In this war, we are instructed to keep our eyes fixed on Jesus Christ, *"the author and perfecter of our faith, who for the joy set before Him endured the cross, despising the shame, and has sat down at the right hand of the throne of God"* (Heb. 12:2). It's the suffering of Jesus that Peter emphatically encourages the disciples whom he is writing to return to in their minds. As they encounter their fiery trials, persecutions, and sufferings, they allow the sufferings of Christ to be the anchor in their minds of what great price has been paid and the victory such suffering has already brought to those who are faithful soldiers.

Along with the sufferings of Christ, in 1 Peter 5:9 Peter instructs the recipients of this letter to remember *"the same experiences of suffering are being accomplished by your brethren who are in the world."* In other words, we are not alone in what we are going through. The Hebrew writer utilized the same psychological recentering of perspective when in chapter 11 we read,

> *And what more shall I say? For time will fail me if I tell of Gideon, Barak, Samson, Jephthah, of David and Samuel and the prophets, who by faith conquered kingdoms, performed acts of righteousness, obtained promises, shut the mouths of lions, quenched the power of fire, escaped the edge of the sword, from weakness were made strong, became mighty in war, put foreign*

armies to flight. Women received back their dead by resurrection; and others were tortured, not accepting their release, so that they might obtain a better resurrection; and others experienced mockings and scourgings, yes, also chains and imprisonment. They were stoned, they were sawn in two, they were tempted, they were put to death with the sword; they went about in sheepskins, in goatskins, being destitute, afflicted, ill-treated (men of whom the world was not worthy), wandering in deserts and mountains and caves and holes in the ground. And all these, having gained approval through their faith, did not receive what was promised, because God had provided something better for us, so that apart from us they would not be made perfect. Therefore, since we have so great a cloud of witnesses surrounding us, let us also lay aside every encumbrance and the sin which so easily entangles us, and let us run with endurance the race that is set before us." Hebrews 11:32-12:1

It is this knowledge that others are enduring the same sufferings and persecutions for surrendering to Christ that is to help encourage the disciples who received the letter from Peter and indeed to all who follow Christ to this day. When we think we are alone in this fight, we focus on mour demise instead of our God who is bigger and more able than even the strongest army of darkness's physical or spiritual forces. This is exactly what Elijah needed to be reminded of in 1 Kings 19, and it's what you and I must keep in mind as we feel the pain of the suffering. We know sufferings are temporary; however, just as the disciples in the day of Peter's writing needed to be reminded, we do as well.

The truth is God does care for us (1 Pet. 5:6). The fact that Christians suffer for His name's sake doesn't change this. As worldly, carnal knowledge and suspicions drive critics to question why God doesn't stop the suffering and persecution against His followers, those of us who have surrendered through submission in humbling ourselves under the mighty hand of God have embraced His will. We live with the understanding that if God wills for suffering to occur in our lives, then so be it (1 Pet. 3:17). If we do suffer for Christ, we are not ashamed, and we glory in the name of God (1 Pet. 3:16).

WHEN WE THINK WE ARE ALONE IN THIS FIGHT, WE FOCUS ON OUR DEMISE INSTEAD OF OUR GOD.

If the mighty hand of God allows suffering and persecution to occur, we will simply fight for His cause by remaining faithful, not merely in our words but also in the lives we surrender daily. After all, the sufferings are only for a little while. The glory God will bestow upon us is eternal (1 Pet. 5:10). Therefore, we live and—if necessary—die with the same theme as Peter used in his conclusion, *"To Him be dominion forever and ever.* Amen" (1 Pet. 5:11).

✪ FIELD NOTES » SURRENDER TO HIS MIGHTY HAND

1. While considering the charge of the Light Brigade, what does it take for a soldier to charge into a scenario where suffering and death seem imminent? Briefly discuss or write down character traits, mental traits, and training that must be present.

2. Since we must surrender to the mighty hands of God, what is your understanding of this phrase? What is it about the hands of God that makes it easier to place yourself under? If you don't place yourself under the mighty hand of God, what will the outcome be?

3. What is your understanding of humility? Briefly consider what this would look like in the life of a genuinely humble man. How do you measure up when it comes to the trait of humility? What is your biggest struggle to being a humble man? What advice would you give to another who asks you how to become more humble?

4. Are "avoiding" and "resisting" the same thing? If so, in what ways? If not, how do they differ? To truly surrender to God, we must be men who "resist" the devil. In what areas of your life do you find it most difficult to resist the devil? How does knowing the devil is looking to devour you impact and affect you, the energy you put forth in resisting him, and the way you guard and watch over your family and home?

5. Surrendering to God is not only about laying down your weapons against Him. It's about considering His purpose and pursuit and making those yours. It's about understanding He is the commanding officer; therefore, you, as the soldier, are on the receiving end of orders, not the giving side. As you close this book, can you say you've truly surrendered to God in every aspect? If not, why not? What is holding you back? If you have, what struggles must you fight against to stay that way? What advice would you give to another man struggling to surrender his life to God fully?

AS THIS BOOK ENDS,
MAY YOUR SURRENDER CONTINUE

CHAPTER 1 »» SURRENDER TO HIS GOSPEL

1. "Surrender Quotes (689 Quotes)." Goodreads, Goodreads, https://www.goodreads.com/quotes/tag/surrender.

2. "Surrender." *Merriam-Webster*, Merriam-Webster, https://www.merriam-webster.com/dictionary/surrender.

3. Tacitus, Cornelius. "The Second Battle of Cremona the Histories by Cornelius Tacitus -Book Three (1 -35)." *The Second Battle of Cremona: The Histories by Cornelius Tacitus*, https://www.ourcivilisation.com/smartboard/shop/tacitusc/histries/chap10.htm.

CHAPTER 2 »» SURRENDER TO HIS PURPOSE

1. 1 Wellman, Pastor Jack. "54 Quotes about Surrender." *ChristianQuotes.info*, 29 Dec. 2015, https://www.christianquotes.info/quotes-by- topic/quotes-about-surrender/

2. 2 James Thacher, *A Military Journal during the American Revolutionary War, from 1775 to 1783....* (Boston: Richardson and Lord, 1823), 345–48. https://archive.org/details/militaryjournal00thac/page/344

3. 3 Markus, Ph.D., Donalee. "The Power of Words." *Psychology Today*, Sussex Publishers, 23 Aug. 2023, https://www.psychologytoday.com/us/ blog/designs-strong-minds/202208/the-power-words.

4. Zodhiates, Spiros. "Possession." The Complete Word Study Dictionary: New Testament, AMG Publishers, Chattanooga, TN, 2000.

5. Zodhiates, "Proclaim."

6. Zodhiates.

7. Zodhiates, "Blaspheme."

8. "Founders Online: To George Washington from Charles Cornwallis, 17 October 1781." *National Archives and Records Administration*, Nation- al Archives and Records Administration, https://founders.archives.gov/documents/Washington/99-01-02-07184.

CHAPTER 3 〉〉〉 SURRENDER TO HIS PURSUITS

1. 1 Wellman, Pastor Jack. "54 Quotes about Surrender." *ChristianQuotes.info*, 29 Dec. 2015, https://www.christianquotes.info/ quotes-by-topic/quotes-about-surrender/.

2. Russell, Shahan. "In WW2, This USAAF Pilot Defected, He Flew His P-38 to Milan & Joined the SS." *Warhistoryonline*, 12 Oct. 2017, https://www.warhistoryonline.com/world-war-ii/usaaf-pilot-defected-flew-his-p38-to-milan-and-joined-the-ss-copy.html?safari=1&D4c=1&D_4_6cALL=1&D_4_6_10cALL=1&A1c=1.

3. Zodhiates Spiros. "Harmonious." *The Complete Word Study Dictionary: New Testament*, AMG Publishers, Chattanooga, TN

4. Zodhiates, "Sympathetic."

5. Zodhiates, "Brotherly."

6. Zodhiates, "Kindhearted."

7. Kittel, Gerhard, et al. *Theological Dictionary of the New Testament: Abridged in One Volume*, W.B. Eerdmans, Grand Rapids, MI,1985, p. 1152.

8. Zodhiates, "Righteousness."

CHAPTER 4 〉〉〉 SURRENDER TO HIS WILL

1. "Glory of God Quotes: A-Z Quotes." *AZ Quotes*, https://www.azquotes.com/quotes/topics/glory-of-god.html?p=2.

2. Meiggs, Russell. "Alcibiades." *Encyclopedia Britannica*, Encyclopedia Britannica, Inc., 11 Feb. 2023, https://www.britannica.com/biography/Alcibiades-Athenian-politician-and-general.

3. Denova, Rebecca. "Flavius Josephus." *World History Encyclopedia*, https://www.worldhistory.org#Organization, 11 Feb. 2023, https://www.worldhistory.org/Flavius_Josephus/.

4. "Ashikaga Takauji." *Encyclopedia of World Biography*. Encyclopedia.com. 4 Feb. 2023 <https://www.encyclopedia.com>.

5. Elhassan, Khalid. "12 Generals You Won't Believe Switched Sides and Defected to the Enemy." *History Collection*, 2 May 2021, https://historycollection.com/12-generals-switched-sides-turned-coat/11/.

6. Britannica, The Editors of Encyclopedia. "Benedict Arnold". Encyclopedia Britannica, 10 Jan. 2023, https://www.britannica.com/biography/Ben- edict-Arnold. Accessed 13 February 2023.

7. Elhassan.

8. Zodhiates, Spiros, et al. "Conformed." *Complete Word Study Dictionary*, OakTree Software, Altamonte Springs, FL, 2016.

9. Zodhiates, "Sensuality."

10. Zodhiates, "Lust."

11. Zodhiates, "Drunkenness."

12. Zodhiates, "Carousing."

13. Zodhiates, "Drinking Parties."

14. Kittel, Gerhard, et al. *Theological Dictionary of the New Testament: Abridged in One Volume*, W.B. Eerdmans, Grand Rapids, MI, 1985, pp. 202–203.

15. Zodhiates, "Surprised."

16. Zodhiates, "Malign."

17. Zodhiates, "Hospitable."

18. Zodhiates, "Blessed."

19. Zodhiates, "Glorify."

20. Zodhiates, "Entrust."

CHAPTER 5 ›› SURRENDER TO HIS MIGHTY HAND

1. Wellman, Pastor Jack. "16 Awesome Quotes about Surrendering to God." *ChristianQuotes.info*, 1 Dec. 2019, https://www.christianquotes.info/ top-quotes/16-awesome-quotes-about-surrendering-to-god/.

2. Lord Tennyson, Alfred. "The Charge of the Light Brigade." Poetry Foundation, *Poetry Foundation*, https://www.poetryfoundation.org/poems/45319/the-charge-of-the-light-brigade.

3. Bunting, Tony. "Battle of Balaklava." *Encyclopedia Britannica*, Encyclopædia Britannica, Inc., https://www.britannica.com/ event/Battle-of-Balaklava.

4. Comfort, Philip W., and Walter A. Elwell. *Tyndale Bible Dictionary*, Tyndale House Publishers Inc, U.S.A. Illinois, Wheaton, 2001, 9

5. Zodhiates, Spiros. "Witness." *The Complete Word Study Dictionary: New Testament*, AMG Publishers, Chattanooga, TN, 2000.

6. Zodhiates, "Clothe."

7. Zodhiates, "Humility."

8. Zodhiates, "Sober."

9. Zodhiates, "Adversary."

10. Zodhiates, "Devil."

11. Zodhiates, "Alert."

12. Zodhiates.

13. Zodhiates, "Resist."

www.ingramcontent.com/pod-product-compliance
Lightning Source LLC
Chambersburg PA
CBHW041130110526
44592CB00020B/2751